"What fun to read *The*

What fun to read *The Joy of Hospitality!* Through their conversation-over-tea style, Vonette Bright and Barbara Ball provide practical how-to's for novices and creative, fresh ideas for seasoned hostesses. This book is a welcome addition to my library.

Mrs. David (Robyne) Bryant
Co-founder, Concerts of Prayer International

My husband, Dennis, and I have been firsthand recipients of Vonette Bright's hospitality. No one makes you feel more at home than Vonette. I'm thrilled that she and Barbara Ball will come alongside many as they mentor through these pages!

Barbara Rainey
Co-founder, FamilyLife Ministry

This wonderful book contains an incredible method of fulfilling Jesus' Great Commission. To reach out in love to the lost in such a friendly way is doable by every Christian woman who cares. Read it and use it.

Evelyn Christianson
Speaker, Best-selling Author

In our hectic, tired generation, when we scarcely have time to do more than brush past the lost people in our lives, Vonette and Barbara encourage us to rediscover the "forgotten ministry" of hospitality. *The Joy of Hospitality* is full of scriptural insights, helpful illustrations, and practical suggestions for cultivating a lifestyle of sharing Jesus through an open heart and home.

Nancy Leigh DeMoss
Life Action Ministries

For years I have been the joyful recipient of the thoughtful, warm hospitality of Vonette and Barbara. They are well worth learning from because few people do it better than they do.

> **Ney Bailey**
> Speaker, Author

If you don't think you have a creative bone in your body, this book is for you. Written for singles as well as marrieds, it encourages all of us to reach out with confidence to a self-centered world.

> **Anne Miller**
> Chairperson, Women of Vision, Dallas

This book has brought fresh inspiration. Only eternity will tell how many people will be reached for Christ through these practical, durable ideas. I highly recommend it!

> **Mrs. Adrian (Joyce) Rogers**
> Author, Pastor's Wife, Women's Ministry Leader

It is a delight to read a book on hospitality that is both practical and encouraging. Vonette Bright and Barbara Ball do an excellent job of challenging women to share God's love in their neighborhoods. This is essential reading for all who want to experience the "joy of hospitality."

> **Mrs. Josh (Dottie) McDowell**
> Author, Speaker

I have had many opportunities to use my home to share the "good news" and am delighted to recommend this book. It is chock-full of wonderful ideas and practical tips.

> **Mrs. Norm (Bobbe) Evans**
> Pro Athletes Outreach

VONETTE BRIGHT
& BARBARA BALL

PUBLICATIONS
A MINISTRY OF CAMPUS CRUSADE FOR CHRIST

The Joy of Hospitality: Fun Ideas for Evangelistic Entertaining

Published by

New*Life* Publications

A ministry of Campus Crusade for Christ

100 Sunport Lane

Orlando, FL 32809

Design and typesetting by Genesis Publications.

Cover design by David Marty.

Photography © by FoodPix.

Printed in the United States of America.

Library of Congress Cataloging-in-Publication Data

Bright, Vonette Z.
    The joy of hospitality : fun ideas for evangelistic entertaining /
    Vonette Bright and Barbara Ball.
        p. cm.
    Includes bibliographical references.
    ISBN 1-56399-079-2 (hardcover) — ISBN 1-56399-057-1 (trade paper)
    1. Evangelistic work.   2. Hospitality—Religious aspects—Christianity.   3. Entertaining.
4. Witness bearing (Christianity).
I. Ball, Barbara. II. Title.
BV3793.B65   1996
269'.2—dc20   95-46627
                                                                       CIP

Unless otherwise noted, Scripture quotations are from the *New International Version*, ©1973, 1984 by the International Bible Society. Published by Zondervan Bible Publishers, Grand Rapids, Michigan.

Scripture quotations designated TLB are from *The Living Bible,* ©1971 by Tyndale House Publishers, Wheaton, Illinois.

Scripture quotations designated Amplified are taken from *The Amplified New Testament,* ©1958, 1987 by the Lockman Foundation, La Habra, California.

Scripture quotations designated NASB are from the *New American Standard Bible,* ©1960, 1962, 1963, 1968, 1971, 1972, 1975, 1977 by the Lockman Foundation, La Habra, California.

For more information, write:

Life Ministries—P.O. Box 40, Flemington Markets, N5W 2129, Australia
Campus Crusade for Christ of Canada—Box 300, Vancouver, B.C., V6C 2X3, Canada
Campus Crusade for Christ—Fairgate House, King's Road, Tyseley, Birmingham,
    B11 2AA, England
Campus Crusade for Christ—P.O. Box 8786, Auckland, New Zealand
Campus Crusade for Christ—Alexandra, P.O. Box 0205, Singapore, 9115, Singapore
Great Commission Movement of Nigeria—P.O. Box 500, Jos, Plateau State Nigeria,
    West Africa
Campus Crusade for Christ International—100 Sunport Lane, Orlando FL 32809, USA

In Memory of Don Tanner
to whom God gave the vision for this book

Within hours after the completion of the manuscript,
Don's last assignment from the Lord, God took him home.

Don Tanner was a godly, gifted editor whose wise council
encouraged many authors in the writing and publishing
of scores of books. His legacy will continue to generations
yet unborn.

In appreciation and gratitude,

Vonette Bright
Barbara Ball

Contents

Acknowledgments

This book has been a cooperative effort of many people. Don Tanner, director of NewLife Publications, was one of the first to get excited about the possibilities of this book and suggested that Barbara and I write it together. We thank Don for his "push" and for his editing skills. Joette Whims spent many hours reading handwritten chapters, transcribing tapes, picking our brains, and using her skills to help complete this manuscript. Without her, we could never have met the publishing deadline. We also wish to thank Jean Bryant and Lynn Copeland for their work editing the final draft and Michelle Treiber for her assistance in the project.

Many others have contributed their expertise. Nancy Wilson of Student Venture and Bill Logan, youth pastor at Immanuel Baptist Church, gave us valuable input on the youth chapter. Joyce Bademan added her extensive experience to help us with the chapter, "Enjoying Christmas Parties." Morris and Linda Erickson, Child Evangelism Fellowship state directors for North Dakota, suggested material for the children's chapter. In various places, we have referred to or adapted material from several ministries within Campus Crusade, including the Executive Ministry, ChurchLIFE, and the Campus Ministry. We want to thank the staff members who have been so generous in sharing their strategies with us. Barbara and I also appreciate the time given by the Women Today staff who supported our efforts.

Our greatest debt of gratitude goes to our husbands, Howard Ball and Bill Bright, who believed in us, made us ministry partners, and for this project have freed us from a number of responsibilities, allowing us to write and edit. They are our most enthusiastic supporters and fans.

We are grateful to each person who contributed and pray that God will use our efforts to further His kingdom and for His glory!

Life Sharing

*Opening your home in joyful
hospitality is an effective way
to build bridges to those
who need Christ.*

CHAPTER 1

We Didn't Know Evangelism Could Be Fun!

Vonette

NOT LONG ago, my dear friend Lois Eger wrote a birthday poem and called me a "party girl." It's true! I love a party. I like getting people together—not only for fun, but also for a purpose. I like to see people enjoy themselves, relax, laugh, develop friendships, feel important and loved, and most of all, to be introduced to Jesus Christ. When they are blessed, I always feel rewarded. And I've discovered that one of the most effective ways to reach out to others is through joyful hospitality in our homes, in our neighborhoods, and where we work and play.

Everyone likes a party. Mention the word and eyes light up. At the same time, most Christians want to reach out to their friends, neighbors, coworkers, and loved ones with the good news of Jesus. It seems like a great combination for evangelism.

But many Christians don't know how to reach out, or they feel overwhelmed by the methods of evangelism they've tried. Others worry about the high cost of entertaining or fear the responsibility

13

of planning and hosting an event. Perhaps you have experienced some of these feelings.

Yet God honors all kinds of hospitality. Luncheons for a few or for hundreds of guests, lively children's parties, energetic youth get-togethers, sporting events, and neighborhood coffees are all effective ways to help others discover a new life in Christ.

Life Sharing

This is why Barbara and I have written this book. We want to present a simple, adaptable way to share your spiritual life by hosting evangelistic events where you live, work, and play. We will show you how to "give a cup of cold water" in the name of Christ and how to help non-Christians receive living water and begin growing into fruitful disciples of the Lord Jesus. We call this "life sharing," and have found it to be a fun, easy way to share our faith.

Jesus said, "I no longer call you servants, because a servant does not know his master's business. Instead, I have called you friends, for everything that I learned from my Father I have made known to you" (John 15:15). As Christians, our mission is to share the friendship we have with Jesus with those who don't know Him personally and then help them begin to grow in their new faith.

I began at an early age to see how rewarding a life of sharing can be. When I was growing up, Mother and Dad loved to invite friends into our home. Some of my earliest recollections are of Mother teaching me to pass out napkins, to wait to be served last, and to pay attention to details that make guests feel comfortable and appreciated.

In those days the population of Coweta, Oklahoma, our little town, was only 1,500, but we enjoyed an amazing number of formal events. Several professional couples had moved to the community, and our town enjoyed preserving some of the culture those people brought with them.

As a child, I observed afternoon teas and candlelight dinners. As a teenager, I enjoyed formal parties and looked forward to the ice cream socials and watermelon feeds held by churches and various groups in the summer. Hayrides and barbecues brightened my winters. I was so impressed with these events that I thought, *It'll be so much fun to go to these parties when I'm grown up.*

Home and hospitality were so important to me that I chose to major in home economics in college. At the time, I didn't know how God would use the things I was learning. In fact, I wasn't even sure I was a Christian! Of course, God knew all about me and about the plans He had for my life.

By the time Bill Bright and I were married, the formal entertaining in Coweta had largely subsided. One exception was at my bridal shower. Every woman in town was invited. The hostesses asked me to wear a formal and some of them did, too. What a great time we had! Through this event and others, Bill and I had seen how a home could be used to encourage people, so we wanted God to use ours to bless and enrich the lives of others.

Our Contract

During our second year of marriage, Bill suggested that we sign a contract with God, totally surrendering our lives to Him. Since Bill had signed hundreds of contracts as a businessman, an agreement between us and the Lord seemed reasonable to him.

"Let's write down exactly what we want out of life—our lifetime goals," he suggested, "to remind us that we are committed to working together." I agreed. So later that afternoon we wrote and signed a contract, surrendering our lives completely and irrevocably to the Lord and to each other. That contract has formed the basis of our lives and ministry.

We listed everything we wanted out of this new life. Bill headed his list with "to be a slave of Jesus Christ." My list was more materialistic. (Wouldn't you know!) I wanted a home modest enough to invite a person from skid row (which was part of our ministry at that time) but lovely enough to entertain the President of the United States. That was a tall order!

Initial Attempts

We held our first modest dinner on March 17, 1949. Bill had met a businessman who didn't know Christ and invited him and his wife to be our guests. But I had a problem. After our wedding on December 30, we left for California and honeymooned on the way. Immediately after we arrived in Los Angeles, I accepted a teaching position in the city school district and had just enough time to unpack before starting my new job. Now a few short weeks later, we were going to entertain in our new home!

I had much to learn about what God expects for hospitality. This was my first lesson. As wedding gift suggestions, I had chosen Lenox china, Bavarian crystal, and sterling silver. Bill and I had received generous wedding presents, but not enough to complete place settings for four. I *had* received twelve place settings of green glass "oatmeal china" like those found inside boxes of oatmeal. I soon learned to appreciate that set of "twelve of everything"!

I was elated that my dinner was scheduled on St. Patrick's Day. How appropriate that we had green "china." I placed a white cloth on the table, cut shamrocks from green construction paper for place mats, and used a St. Patrick's Day theme in the centerpiece.

We spent the evening sharing our faith with the businessman and his wife. At that time, Bill and I were very inexperienced in how to lead a person to Christ. Although I don't remember whether they received Him as their Savior that night, I do know they were responsive to what we said. We were thrilled. And I began to understand how to use what we had to honor Christ.

God is gracious! He places no value on our possessions. He doesn't pressure us to perform, or require us to be sophisticated. Instead, He sees our hearts and understands our needs. Through the power of His Holy Spirit, He uses us where we live to help heal the hurts and broken spirits of those who need His love.

I'm so glad He doesn't prefer the rich and famous or consider the poor person more worthy. He loves us as we are, then gives us the power to grow and serve Him with fruitful, holy lives. Relying on His strength and wisdom, I learned confidence in life sharing.

Special Guest

That simple dinner was just the beginning of a ministry for me. In the fall, Bill and I became involved in the 1949 Billy Graham Los

Angeles Crusade. At the beginning of the several-week crusade, Bill said, "Vonette, I'm impressed by how you make people feel comfortable in our home. Would it be all right if I invited Billy Graham to dinner?"

My first thought was, *My oatmeal china!* "Could we buy another set of dishes?" I asked timidly.

Bill laughed. "Sounds like a good idea."

When Billy Graham accepted, Bill and I were excited about entertaining him and naive about what that meant. We bought Franciscan pottery from an outlet store. The set was gray and maroon and didn't match anything we had. The plates were so huge that they required an exorbitant amount of food to fill them.

But God's plan was not for a formal, silver-and-candles meal with me presiding as an elegant hostess. Instead, He arranged just the right kind of atmosphere for a special guest.

At that time, our home was a small two-bedroom English cottage at the back of a larger house in the Hollywood hills. The cottage had a lot of charm, but now I realize that it was not what most people would consider appropriate for entertaining the President of the United States—or Billy Graham.

Bill and I anticipated serving a small party, including Billy and an assistant or two, after the meeting. I stayed home that night to finish preparing the meal while Bill attended the service.

When he returned, he brought Billy's entire team—including Cliff Barrows, Grady and T. W. Wilson, George Beverly Shay, Jerry Bevins, Chuck Turner, George Wilson, and the organist and pianist—plus Stewart and Susie Hamlin.

Susie was a marvelous Christian woman who had been praying for her husband, a western radio entertainer. Stewart had not received Christ as his Savior, and she was thrilled that he had this opportunity to be with Billy Graham.

Susie realized my food-shortage predicament and pitched in to help me prepare more food. Where it all came from, I'll never know! But we had plenty to eat—in spite of those huge plates. And Grady and T. W. Wilson's great jokes made the evening hilarious!

None of us forgot that meal. Certainly Stewart, whose business was storytelling, saw firsthand that the Christian life is not straight-laced, sober, or sad. A few days later, Stewart committed his life to Christ and gave his testimony at the crusade. I like to believe that our simple hospitality may have helped make a difference in his life. We have been friends of their family ever since.

Changing Lives

Does using your home to share your faith intrigue you? You can experience fun and fellowship, and see people come to know Christ. What an exciting combination!

In this book, Barbara and I want to show you how you can begin your ministry of evangelistic hospitality. Whether you're male or female, young or old, married or single, this way of sharing your faith in Christ can work for you. We'll give you step-by-step help on how to plan and host such events as:

* Women's brunches and coffees
* Men's events
* Couples socials
* Singles gatherings
* Video presentations
* Youth get-togethers
* Children's parties

To help you host life-sharing events, we'll show you how to present your testimony or introduce a speaker. You'll also learn how to help new believers and interested Christians get involved in small-group Bible studies. We will give some creative ideas to help you hold festive events through your church ministry, neighborhood outreach, or at your workplace.

After many years of ministry, I'm even more excited about how life sharing can change lives, families, and neighborhoods! As Christians, we have the privilege of offering that cup of cold water to those who are thirsty for God. And we can do it right where we are—at home, at work, or at play!

CHAPTER 2

How God Used a
Shy Person Like Me

Barbara

MY EXPERIENCES with life sharing are very different from Vonette's. She is such a dynamic, outgoing person that I could never be like her.

At one time I admired Vonette so much that I tried to be just like her. But as I began maturing in my faith, I realized that God had created me as a unique personality and that He had a plan specifically for *me*. I made peace with myself and stopped frustrating the Holy Spirit's work in my life by trying to emulate Vonette. I could learn from her, and did, but I also needed to be open to what God wanted me to do.

Years ago, I would never have dreamed that I could do the things I'm doing today. When I look back on my life, I can still see myself at twenty-nine—a shy, lonely, negative, angry woman. What a difference! I am still shy, but now I choose to walk in the Spirit of Christ and experience His love, joy, and peace and His patience with others. If I had remained as I was, I would never have found release from the bondage of my own limitations nor learned to appreciate the value of interesting people. I now have many new friends, friends with varied backgrounds and different types of experiences, and of different ages.

I feel so blessed. Eva Brandt, wife of psychologist Henry Brandt, once told me, "Barbara, you are becoming what you will become—and increasingly more as you grow older."

Because of Christ, I have a goal for my life: to be a loving, happy, fruitful, fun-to-be-with older woman. I agree with John 15:5, which says, "Apart from me you can do nothing." Only God's power could change me so much and make me an effective witness where I live.

"I Think I Can Do It!"

You may wonder how all this happened. The changes occurred because I chose to be available to God's leading. And sometimes that was difficult.

When my husband, Howard, and I joined the staff of Campus Crusade in 1963, Dr. Bright encouraged us to move to Arrowhead Springs, California. I panicked. I wanted God's will, but not a move! I enjoyed the security of living near parents, siblings, and good friends. I loved our large colonial home.

So when we arrived at the Arrowhead Springs grounds, I didn't have a good attitude. In fact, I hated the four-room bunga- low that was to be our new home.

But the Lord wouldn't let me harbor wrong attitudes. He reminded me of my dissatisfaction until I finally said, "Lord, I can't imagine even liking this place. If you give me a love for it, then I'll know You are real."

Since Howard and I didn't have enough money to remodel, we cleaned and made do with what we had. Within a few weeks, the bungalow began to feel like home and my love for it budded and grew. We stayed in that bungalow for three years—and enjoyed some of the best times of our lives there.

While living on the campus, I spent time with Vonette and with other staff members. At first, I didn't think I fit in with the staff. They were excited about sharing their faith, but I wasn't!

Little by little, though, I began to understand Dr. Bright's message on the presence of the Holy Spirit in a believer's life and how we can minister effectively only through His power. But I still couldn't do much because I was limiting God's work in my life.

Thus, Vonette became a gift to me from the Lord. She kept telling me, "One day we'll be speaking and teaching others together."

I responded, "I just don't see myself doing that."

But she was loving, kind, and very understanding. (I will always be grateful for that.) She didn't preach at me or push me into something that I was not ready to do. She simply came alongside and encouraged me. She began by asking me to go with her on speaking engagements and pray for her and the audience while she spoke. I felt comfortable doing that and enjoyed the conversations with people at the events. During these times Vonette and I often found time to shop and to talk on the way home.

Finally, I felt confident enough to say to her, "Vonette, I think I can do what you are doing."

She took note.

Stepping Out in Faith

One day, Vonette realized that she had double speaking engagements and suggested that I take her place for one of them. Here was my chance. But I was afraid!

Since no one else could fill in for Vonette, I agreed to go. When I arrived, the hostess happily greeted me, but when I told her that Vonette couldn't come, her face darkened with disappointment. (I made a quick, wise decision—I didn't tell her this was my first time to speak.)

I had observed Vonette's outline in evangelistic settings. She often gave her personal testimony and a clear presentation of the gospel. I followed her plan as well as I could.

I don't remember much about that day. My memory was probably fuzzy because of my nervousness. But God was there, convincing, convicting, loving those women to Himself! I was simply His vessel. When five women indicated that they had received Christ, I couldn't believe it. God actually had used a shy person like me!

When I returned to the hotel, I excitedly shared with Dr. Bright, Vonette, and Howard what had happened. Dr. Bright has a great sense of humor. "Well," he chuckled, "Barbara Billy Graham Ball."

We all laughed. But I realized I was on a new adventure. *God would use me to touch lives!* I had always thought that only those with outgoing personalities could be effective speakers or good at sharing their faith in Christ. But now I had experienced a supernatural afternoon. I was lifted up out of my limitations. I was freed from myself.

Vonette has continued to encourage me through the years by her own life. She is practical, fun, always looking for a new way or venture in which to share Christ. I lift up no person. I know well that Jesus is the only worthy object of my faith. But I am so grateful that Vonette came alongside me!

Unexpected Results

After my first speaking opportunity, I concluded that this method of sharing Christ could encourage others to reach out. I typed up helpful tips for being a hostess. When other women read them, they expressed interest. When Vonette heard what I had done, she suggested we put the guidelines into a booklet, which we did, and we called it *Evangelistic Entertaining*.

That booklet, written twenty-five years ago, thrust me into a vital ministry. Many people in Campus Crusade's lay ministry helped us by furnishing additional information for hosting evangelistic events. What great fun we had working together with our different gifts and abilities!

Imagine! Me, a shy, inhibited person becoming involved with an evangelistic ministry and finding more joy, satisfaction, and results than I ever could have dreamed of.

How did this happen? Through God's gracious leading and patient work in my life.

Where did I find my avenue of special interest? In helping and encouraging other women to reach out to their neighbors with a simple coffee/tea ministry. In the past few years, I have come a long way in learning how to love my neighbors, share my faith with them, and invite them to reach out in their neighborhoods, too.

Imagine how I felt one day when I realized that in my busyness of ministry, I was *not* doing what I encouraged others to do. I didn't know my own neighbors. I had become a "professional" teacher. I was sharing with Christians how to reach out, but was too busy to talk to my own neighbors!

I discovered this when I planned a Christmas coffee at my home. By this time, Howard and I had moved from our Arrowhead Springs bungalow into a house that we purchased in San Bernardino. I sent twenty-five invitations, but only three of my neighbors came. True, small groups are fine with the Lord. But my neighbors didn't come because they didn't know me and were apprehensive about what I was doing.

Right then, I decided to get to *know* my neighbors. I asked the Lord what I could do to meet them, and He impressed me to consider what I do best.

I love to make bread, so I began taking a loaf to each home and staying to visit. I continued baking and visiting my neighbors until I built friendship bridges to them.

I also reached out to young girls in our neighborhood. They admired my long, polished fingernails so I invited them to a once-a-week nail clinic. We ate cookies, and I fixed little manicure sets for them. "My father gave me a beautiful manicure set in a black velvet case when I was young," I told them. "Taking care of my nails helped me break my habit of biting them."

The girls came for several weeks, and we had such fun. How did God use that? When we held a New Year's Open House, Irving and Mildred, my Jewish neighbors, arrived thanking me for being so kind to their children. From that evening, I also became involved with their son's Bar Mitzvah and their daughter's Bat Mitzvah.

One day, I invited Mildred to come with me to hear my good friend Ney Bailey speak. Mildred came, and she heard my friend's testimony and the gospel. Mildred obviously enjoyed the event, and she and I have continued our friendship to this day.

After two years in that neighborhood, four torrential rain storms drove mud down from the mountainside, and our entire area was forced to move. We all helped and loved each other. The local newspapers printed an article and photo of my three friends and me praying for our neighbors. The article was called "And Barbara, We Will Pray for You!" Most important, I was able to witness to many of those neighbors. That's how I began sharing Christ as a way of life!

Open Doors

Because of the mudslide, the Lord gave Howard and me a special new home. It was just what we wanted and in the neighborhood where we wanted to live. But the house hadn't been painted in thirty years and needed a lot of work, so we remodeled and redecorated.

The Lord began to open doors for ministry. As a result of redecorating, the house was placed on the Annual Lawyers' Wives Home Tour. Our neighbors came for the tour, and Howard and I were able to welcome them into our home.

During the Christmas holidays, I decided to invite my neighbors over for brunch. I was excited about this new opportunity to spread God's love and forgiveness. I wrote invitations and personally delivered them because I hadn't met everyone yet.

When I came to a house in the middle of the block, a woman cautiously opened the door. I explained about the brunch and offered her an invitation. She took it, then curtly informed me, "We don't do *this* in *this* neighborhood."

For a moment, I felt rejected and wondered what to do. "I'm sorry," I replied, "but I've already passed out several invitations. I'll have to go ahead and have the brunch anyway."

And by faith, I did just that. My two neighbors on either side helped me plan and prepare. Twenty-six women came—among them the one who said, "We don't do this…"

We ate and shared Christmas traditions, and then I introduced a friend, Helen Wilson, who shared her personal testimony for ten minutes. The brunch ended on such a high note that two neighbors who helped me host the event were thrilled. They kept exclaiming, "Carol enjoyed herself so much! And so did her friend, Jennifer!"

A small beginning toward a changed neighborhood! We lived in that house thirteen years. After the second year of the now-traditional brunch, a doctor's wife of another faith suggested inviting our husbands. So the men came that third year. While we visited, the doctor proposed having a progressive dinner for couples. During the remaining time Howard and I stayed in that area, we held a dinner every year.

Those brunches and dinners helped build a fruitful ministry. As Howard and I held Bible studies, some of our neighbors received Christ while others grew in their faith. We all learned to love and appreciate each other. Eventually, Howard and I sold our home and moved to Winter Park, Florida, near Campus Crusade's World Headquarters in Orlando.

As we were preparing to move, the doctor and his wife gave a going-away party for us because, they said, Howard and I had helped the neighbors get to know and care about each other! Just recently, I received a note from the doctor's wife telling me that the friendliness among our former neighbors had continued. The groundwork has been laid, and who knows what God will do?

More Opportunities

At this point, you may be thinking, *I could never do this in my neighborhood. It's a lot different from yours.* But it isn't the kind of people who live close to us that determines whether we minister or not; it's the great God whom we serve. His plan is to meet people where they are, then address their needs. I realize that some neighborhoods or workplaces are more open than others. But each has men and women who are hurting and who will open their hearts to Christ when we approach them with God's love. We just need to be aware of His leading in our lives. That's the confidence I had while packing our belongings for the move across country.

We soon discovered our Florida neighborhood was completely different. As we moved in, some of the neighbors welcomed us with wonderful food dishes. Out of appreciation, we invited them to an open house and met most of them.

When Easter approached, I invited the women to an Easter brunch. We ate, then each person shared her background and how many children or grandchildren she had. As each woman described herself, I discovered that these women had lived in this neighborhood for years. I began to realize that we lived in a unique neighborhood—these women were listening and concerned for each other.

I closed with a short, inspirational reading that had a God-directed conclusion. When I finished, the women asked for copies. As they left, they bubbled with the comfort and joy of getting to know each other.

On the first day of fall, I invited the women in again for a cup of coffee and a muffin. We all enjoyed our time together. As the morning ended, I told them I had decided to teach a six-week Bible study and invited them to come. Six of them responded. During those studies, we appreciated being with each other and sharing what we had learned.

Early in the Christmas season, I told the women about our neighborhood in southern California and how much we had enjoyed our progressive dinners. All six women agreed that they would like to do the same in this neighborhood. Two offered to open their homes. Many of the neighbors participated. We served appetizers in one home, salad and entrees in another. One of our neighbors, who sang with the Bach Choral, agreed to sing at the dinner, and her selections fit in beautifully with the Christmas theme. The evening closed with dessert in our home.

Following the dinner, we received many thank you's. Now, as caring friends, we know each other better and are even more concerned for each other. Howard and I have more freedom to share Christ, and I began another Bible study because more people wanted to come.

Our latest event was a going-away party for our next-door neighbors. We hosted a casual tail-gate party at 5 o'clock on the day their furniture was packed and ready to go. The neighbor across the street parked her van in her driveway. The back end was loaded with boxes of barbecue from a restaurant, chocolate cake, soft drinks, and coffee. Other neighbors and friends brought lawn chairs. The meal was easy to put together and the fellowship was relaxing. But more than that, the going-away party was a touch of love to this couple. They commented, "This meal eases the pain of moving away after thirty years in the same neighborhood."

The purpose for life sharing is not always to give an invitation for guests to receive Christ. Sometimes, we can demonstrate what life in Christ is about: loving others and seeing positive changes in people and in neighborhoods.

I have learned through the years that there is no right plan, no perfect strategy to reach people. Each person is unique, and everyone needs the love, care, and concern that fits his or her personality and situation. Meeting these needs is accomplished only when God uses someone who lives under His control and is willing to do His good pleasure.

We should not assume that our neighbors know how to become Christians. There are times when we can be direct, and life sharing helps us present the gospel in a clear, simple way.

We never want to compromise God's eternal message, but the package in which the gospel is presented should always be attractive (2 Corinthians 5:18). Being neighborly causes people to have confidence in you and to be more receptive when a direct gospel message is shared.

Coming Alongside

Reaching out is fun! It's not something you *must* do; it's something you *want* to do. Jesus says, "I will make you fishers of men." Our part is simply to be available. Through the years, I have failed in many attempts to reach out. I often had a purpose that wasn't on God's agenda. But in His grace, He uses anyone who is willing and available. As the saying goes, "Any old bush will do!" The benefit for us is that Christians who make themselves available to God become free in Christ and are released from their own limitations.

Perhaps you feel like I once did—inadequate, shy, and incapable of sharing your faith in Christ. Vonette and I have written this book to come alongside you like she did with me. We want to help you gain confidence in the power of God that can enable you to share His message and encourage new believers to grow in their faith.

In this book, we will not only show you how to plan for and host an event, but we also will give you practical suggestions for helping new believers and Christians mature in their faith. You will learn how to:

- Prepare and give your personal testimony
- Begin and lead a Bible study
- Demonstrate a life-sharing event to introduce others to the concept

No matter where you are in your journey of life sharing, you will discover creative new ways to expand your ministry and help others begin one of their own.

I encourage you to take notes as you read along. Mark ideas that you can apply to your situation. And prepare for an adventure that will have eternal significance in your life and in the lives of many in your neighborhood or workplace. You will find as we have that evangelistic entertaining can be fun.

I encourage you to join Vonette and me in the next step on our journey. You will see how you fit into God's plan as you develop your own ministry of life sharing.

CHAPTER 3

How Do I Fit In?

Vonette

BILL AND I have never lost the desire to make our home a vital part of our ministry. Early in 1951, God gave Bill the vision for Campus Crusade for Christ, which meant reaching out to college students with the gospel. In October of that year, God miraculously orchestrated events so that we were able to lease a large, two-story house in Westwood Village—only one block from the UCLA campus. Now we could open our home to the students.

We started what Campus Crusade now calls College Life Meetings. Bill, our staff members, and I divided into teams to lead meetings at sorority and fraternity houses on Monday nights. We challenged the students to investigate the person and claims of Christ. Following our messages, we invited the men and women to receive Christ. Then we set up appointments for them to meet with us later and invited them to come to our home on Tuesday evening for a large gathering.

The response was wonderful! From the beginning, as many as 150 to 200 students would arrive, filling our living room, hall, stairwell, and the floor. After the meeting, we served refreshments of punch and cookies so the students would linger and we could do what we called "divide and conquer." In other words, we shared our faith with students one to one.

Our house was just beginning to be the home of our dreams. Students loved coming; they felt comfortable visiting with us. Although I still taught school and loved my job, the ministry in our home and on the campus excited me more.

Then something happened that seemed a setback to our ministry. The women who owned the house that we had leased for a year while they vacationed in Brazil wired that they were homesick and asked to break our lease. This meant that after only six months Bill and I had to move, settling farther from the campus. The students now drove to our home on Saturday mornings for prayer and discipleship training, followed by breakfast.

In addition, we had to hold our large meetings in the sorority and fraternity houses. That meant carrying in the punch, cookies, and serving pieces, and setting everything up for the after-meeting snack. Sometimes the houses would cancel events at the last minute. More and more, I realized the advantages of using our home—if we could live near the campus. Real estate near UCLA, however, was expensive and rent was high.

But God wasn't through with our life-sharing ministry. He just planned circumstances differently from what we expected. He had a lot more to teach us about opening our home. He wanted us to experience more of the joys and benefits of using our house and to discover how to meet the needs of non-Christians, providing a nonthreatening atmosphere in which they could examine the claims of Christ.

A Lifestyle of Ministry

Perhaps you have times like I did when you wonder how you can fit into a ministry of life sharing. You may question how using your home—whether simple or elaborate—can really help others. You may doubt that you have what it takes to be hospitable. Or you may fear that having people in your home causes too many problems.

Let me assure you that life sharing can fit anyone's personality, finances, and schedule. It's an adaptable way of witnessing in which almost anyone can be involved. People feel more comfortable in a home, are honored that someone took the time to plan an event for them, and don't sense the uneasiness they may feel in a church.

Let's look at what hospitality really is in God's eyes and how practicing true hospitality will change the way we value and use our homes.

Great Expectations

Justine was throwing together a quick sandwich when the doorbell rang. Stepping quickly into the living room, she glanced out the window and saw her neighbor waiting impatiently at the door. Carol was shifting from one foot to the other, dabbing her eyes with a tissue.

Instinctively, Justine surveyed the room. Yesterday's newspaper was still scattered on the couch. Her briefcase lay open on the end table, and her coat was draped over the chair. A basket of folded laundry sat in the hallway. *I don't have time for this right now,* she thought. *My house is a mess. What does she want?*

Then Carol knocked. Justine hesitated. If she ignored the timid knock, Carol might go away. But Justine had been trying to reach out to Carol for weeks, and this was the first time she had responded to Justine's friendship.

Have you ever been in a situation like this? Maybe the thought of having guests in your home makes you feel self-conscious. What is hospitality, really?

* Making sure you wear a smile when someone is at your door?
* Serving an elaborate meal?
* Inviting people into a beautifully decorated home?

These are only outer trappings. Hospitality comes from the heart. In the Greek language in which the New Testament was written, hospitality is defined as *love for strangers.* I like to give hospitality a broader meaning: showing love to everyone.

Romans 12:10–13 describes how we should treat friends and strangers:

> Be devoted to one another in brotherly love. Honor one another above yourselves. Never be lacking in zeal, but keep

your spiritual fervor, serving the Lord. Be joyful in hope, patient in affliction, faithful in prayer. Share with God's people who are in need. Practice hospitality.

Hospitality is more than entertaining. It is expecting God to do great things through you as you reach out to touch the lives of others. It is focusing on relationships, especially the greatest relationship of all—walking and talking with the Lord Jesus Christ. Hospitality is a natural overflow of Christ's love for us and in us. Our response is to prayerfully consider how we can "love [our] neighbor as [ourselves]" (Matthew 22:39) through our daily lives.

Perhaps you are wondering, *How can I practice hospitality with my busy life? If I add one more meeting, or schedule one more appointment, I'll just explode!*

It's easy to resent guests and the interruption and inconvenience they may cause. But people are more important than circumstances. If we let schedules and a busy life rob us of time for others, we will find ourselves also robbed of the joy and excitement of seeing God work in their lives. At busy times like these, making ourselves available to be used by God in people's lives is even more vital.

True hospitality doesn't wear us out or make us feel pressured; life sharing is not entertaining in our own strength. It flows from a heart full of love for others. Christ's love, which doesn't come from our self-effort, is a work of the Holy Spirit in our lives. The love of Christ is what draws people to God. This love transforms a party or other event into true hospitality.

Hospitality, then, is not an event; it is genuine concern for another's well-being.

Bill has a great and loving heart for people and a desire to introduce others to our Lord. He has always felt that hospitality begins at home.

Recently, Bill and I moved to a condominium area in Orlando. Some time after we became settled, a new family moved into our building. Along with another Christian couple, we decided to have an evening dessert to introduce the new family to others in the complex and to build bridges to evangelism.

We gave out invitations three weeks in advance. Then, shortly before the event, I became ill with a terrible cold. I spent several days in bed and was afraid I would expose my guests to my illness.

Bill suggested that he serve as host for the evening, and our co-host couple agreed to prepare the dessert, so they continued the event as planned. Just before the guests arrived, I aired out the house, then retired to the bedroom.

After greeting the guests, Bill asked everyone to share something special about themselves and how they happened to move into our complex. Then he thanked the Lord for the food and asked God's blessing on each guest. As the dessert was served, people began enjoying conversation. From the way Bill described the fun later, I was sorry I missed the good time.

In the next few days, we received so many wonderful comments on how much people had enjoyed the evening and what a wonderful host Bill was. As his example shows, life sharing is not limited to women. Anyone can have an evangelistic ministry through their home. We need to make opportunities to get acquainted with people and then let them know us.

Hospitality to Strangers

In the Bible, we are instructed to practice hospitality to two kinds of people: other believers and those who do not know the Lord.

Hospitality that we extend to other believers builds up and strengthens the body of Christ. When we come together for vital, loving fellowship, God is glorified because the emphasis is on Him and His great work in our lives. We leave encouraged to grow, to love, to witness, and so on. Fellowship with other believers makes us more fruitful spiritually, and our love for one another proves to nonbelievers that we are Christ's disciples.

However, in this book we will be concerned with "hospitality to strangers"—those who don't yet belong to the family of God. This hospitality demonstrates a love they may have never experienced. It *gives* when the rest of the world *takes*. People notice when we initiate such a loving relationship. As we invite non-Christians into our homes, they will see the difference Christ makes in our lives and in our families.

Indeed, hospitality in the home can be one of the most effective ways to introduce others to Jesus Christ. The relaxed atmosphere opens their hearts to you, and you have the opportunity to identify with your guests in a personal, practical way.

Poor Justine. She was more concerned about the appearance of her house than about the need of her neighbor. People, however, are more important than things, and personal relationships are more important than the surroundings.

You may not feel comfortable inviting people into your home, or you may feel inadequate to handle certain situations or turn a conversation to spiritual matters. In the coming chapters, you will discover just how easy it is to open your home to others as we provide you with tips on how to plan an event effectively and how to share your faith in a non-threatening way.

Whether you are single or married, male or female, live in a house or an apartment, your home is a God-given resource that can be used to touch people in an intimate, personal way. It doesn't matter to God whether your home is elaborate or simple. All He needs is your willingness to love others as He does.

I urge you to expect great things of God as He uses your life and home. No matter what your background, your style of entertaining, or the condition of your house, God can make miracles happen and change people's lives for eternity!

Availability Leads to Ability

Perhaps you agree that any home can be used for life sharing, but you still struggle with problems of confidence or with choosing to do God's will. I can tell you from personal experience that God will enable you to do whatever He asks of you. As we make ourselves available to Him, He will give us the ability, He will control the circumstances, and He will even provide the resources.

We can decide at any time to depend on our own abilities or to trust in the Lord's. If we choose to rely on ourselves, we deny the unlimited power of our Creator-God. That's why many Christians consider witnessing merely a duty. They misunderstand the freedom and power that Christ offers every believer. Consequently, because they minister through self-effort, sharing the gospel becomes a difficult task.

However, when we ask God to lead, guide, and empower us, He accomplishes more through us than we could ever do for ourselves. Jesus says, "Apart from me you can do nothing... If you remain in me and my words remain in you, ask whatever you wish, and it will be given you. This is to my Father's glory, that you bear much fruit, showing yourselves to be my disciples" (John 15:5,7,8). This is Christ's guarantee to those who love Him. He will fill us with His power and help us introduce others to Him.

But how can we make the right choices when our lives are sinful or we don't feel like it? Bill has developed a concept that I've found helpful. It's called Spiritual Breathing. As an exercise in faith, Spiritual Breathing will enable you to continue to experience God's love and forgiveness and the power and control of the Holy Spirit as a way of life.

If you sin by committing a deliberate act of disobedience, breathe spiritually. Exhale by confession. God's Word promises in 1 John 1:9, "If we confess our sins, he is faithful and just and will forgive us our sins and purify us from all unrighteousness." In Greek, the word "confess" (*homologeo*) means to "agree with" or to "say along with." Such agreement involves three considerations.

First, you acknowledge that your sins—which should be named specifically to God—are wrong and are therefore grievous to Him.

Second, you acknowledge that God has already forgiven you through Christ's death and the shedding of His blood on the cross for your sins.

Third, you repent, which means that you change your attitude toward your sin. The power of the Holy Spirit will enable you to change both your attitude and your conduct. Instead of doing what your old sinful nature—your flesh—wants to do, you can do what God wants you to do.

Now inhale by appropriating the fullness of God's Spirit by faith. Trust Him to control and empower you according to His command in Ephesians 5:18 to "be filled with the Spirit," which means to be continually controlled and empowered by the Holy Spirit.

Whatever God commands us to do, He gives us the power to accomplish if we trust and obey Him. Simply ask the Holy Spirit to fill you with His power, and He will! To keep your commitment to life sharing strong and pure, every time you sin, practice Spiritual Breathing.

I challenge you to devote yourself to a ministry of life sharing. You will enjoy getting acquainted with others. Many people will then listen to a clear gospel presentation that they would not hear otherwise. As you make yourself available to God in your sphere of influence, you will gain personal satisfaction. People who visit your home will come to know Him in a personal way. And your family will receive a new vision for what God can do in and through a committed believer.

So can you fit in? Yes! Karen Burton Mains writes in her book, *Open Heart—Open Home,*

> If Christians, corporately, would begin to practice hospitality, we could play significant roles in redeeming our society. There is no better place to be about the redemption of society than in the Christian servant's home; and the more we deal with the captive, the blind, the downtrodden, the more we realize that in this inhospitable world, a Christian home is a miracle to be shared.

Whether you rent or own a house, God has given you a home to share. He will give you the wisdom and love to open it to others. As you do so, you will experience a spiritual adventure that only those who follow Christ can know.

Now let us consider how God uses people like you and me to do the impossible.

CHAPTER 4

The Impact of a
Home Ministry

Barbara

LIFE SHARING produces joy-filled moments. One day I spoke at a coffee in a Dallas, Texas, home. The living room was filled with beautiful women, one of whom was a model. The hostess was very nervous. She wondered how these sophisticated women would react to a simple gospel presentation.

When the time came, I stood and gave my testimony and a short message on how to receive God's love and forgiveness. The guests listened intently, and a few indicated that they wanted to receive Christ as their Savior.

After the coffee, the model approached me with a radiant smile. "Thank you so much for helping me understand more about Jesus Christ!" she exclaimed. "Could you talk to someone else the same way you spoke to us this morning?"

"Sure," I smiled, "but how would *you* explain your new faith to this person?"

She looked away for a moment, pondering her answer. "Well, the other person is my husband. And I would tell him, 'Sugar daddy, you have a brand new mama!'"

I laughed at her vibrant enthusiasm. I could see God's humor at work in her, and I just knew that her husband would understand!

No one is more surprised than I am at being used of God to introduce others to Jesus. Why would He want to love others through me? I am willing, but I'm certainly not perfect. Yet that's the way God works—through Christians who are obedient to His commands.

In both the Old and New Testaments, God gives us examples of how He uses ordinary people like you and me to touch lives. Let's look at some of those examples.

The Impact of a Witness

One Old Testament woman who used her home in ministry was Naomi. She lived in a time of social crisis. Because of the Hebrew nation's disobedience to God through idolatry, He allowed natural elements to oppress the people. During a severe famine, Naomi and Elimelech and their two sons moved to Moab. While living in this foreign land, Elimelech died and Naomi's two sons later married Moabite women—Orpah and Ruth. Eventually, Naomi's sons also died, leaving her without a husband or sons to care for her.

The Bible doesn't tell us what Naomi thought about her new daughters-in-law, but we know that the Moabites were idolaters who worshiped the god Chemosh. Yet Naomi was so compassionate and loving to Orpah and Ruth that when she prepared to return to her own country, they wanted to go with her.

Naomi understood how hard it would be for her daughters-in-law to live in a foreign land, so she encouraged Ruth and Orpah to go back to their own people. However, Naomi had given them such a wonderful picture of the Israelite God, Jehovah, that Ruth abandoned her way of life to follow Naomi.

"Don't urge me to leave you or to turn back from you," Ruth pleaded. "Where you go I will go, and where you stay I will stay. Your people will be my people and your God my God" (Ruth 1:16). Ruth accompanied Naomi to Israel and eventually married Boaz, an Israelite.

I'm sure Naomi didn't foresee the eternal results of her love and witness toward Ruth. As a result of her loving care, Naomi gained a daughter-in-law who not only joined her in worshiping the one true God but who also entered the genetic line of our Lord Jesus Christ.

Jesus Ministered in Homes

The New Testament shows us even more clearly how important it is to open our homes to unbelievers. During His ministry, Jesus made a startling remark: "Foxes have holes and birds of the air have nests, but the Son of Man has no place to lay his head" (Matthew 8:20). Jesus had no home that He could call His own! He had no "base of operations" from which to minister, except at the temple or in someone's home.

Matthew hosted a life-sharing event just after he met Jesus. As a tax collector, he associated with a rough crowd who usually took more than their share of revenues. Few people liked them.

When Matthew invited Jesus and a crowd of friends to his home for a banquet, the religious leaders were incensed. "Why do you eat and drink with tax collectors and 'sinners'?" they criticized.

"It is not the healthy who need a doctor, but the sick," Jesus returned. "I have not come to call the righteous, but sinners to repentance" (Luke 5:30,31). Jesus came to Matthew's home with a purpose—to tell sinners about God's love.

John 4:1–42 relates the story of the Samaritan woman who met Jesus at a well outside a nearby town. Once she realized that He was the Messiah, she left her water jar and ran back to the town, telling her friends about Him. Many townspeople believed in Him because of her testimony! They came out to the well and urged Jesus to stay with them. Jesus stayed two days, and many more people believed in Him.

Jesus enjoyed parties. In fact, He performed His first miracle—changing water into wine—at a wedding in a home in Cana. Because of this miracle, His disciples first believed in Him (John 2:11).

Homes were an important part of Jesus' ministry. He invited Himself to stay at the home of Zacchaeus (Luke 19:5). After Jesus raised Lazarus from the dead, Mary, Martha, and Lazarus invited Him to a supper in their home, and a great multitude came to see Him there (John 12:1–11).

New Testament Ministry

Home ministry was also essential in the development of the new Church that mushroomed after Jesus' resurrection. The first church began meeting in a home. Acts 1:12–14 records the disciples gathering in an upper room of a house to await the coming of the Holy Spirit. Once the Holy Spirit descended upon them, they went out and witnessed to the people who were in Jerusalem.

Other homes quickly opened up for the new churches that sprang up in many towns and cities. Acts 5:42 says, "Day after day, in the temple courts and from house to house, they never stopped teaching and proclaiming the good news that Jesus is the Christ."

The early believers used their homes for worship and evangelism. Can you picture Peter or one of the other disciples entering a home and delivering a sermon? Or sitting down with a family and their friends and telling them about Jesus? Can you visualize the effect that would have had on others around them?

In Acts 20:20,21, Paul says, "You know that I have not hesitated to preach anything that would be helpful to you but have taught you publicly and from house to house. I have declared to both Jews and Greeks that they must turn to God in repentance and have faith in our Lord Jesus." Since these new groups of believers had no buildings in which to meet, their homes became the logical place where churches could grow and minister (Romans 16:3,5; Philemon 1,2).

I like to think that's where life sharing began. Since then, the home has been the center of ministry—especially in areas where believers are persecuted or don't have the freedom to meet in church buildings.

Why are homes so essential? Because no matter how beautiful or warm a church building is, it cannot match the intimacy and comfort that a home offers. God wants us to surrender our residences to Him because He wants to use our resources to introduce people to Him, then lead them to the church. I like what Howard says about our role in witnessing, "The Lord never told the world to go to the church. He told the church to go to the world." Proverbs 3:33 promises: "He blesses the home of the righteous." When we make our homes available for His use, He blesses us.

One of the benefits of a life-sharing ministry is hearing the results of lives that have been changed. Let me share the stories of three who have experienced this adventure. The first is by my husband, Howard. He and I have worked together in couples' events for many years. His enthusiasm for life sharing has been an inspiration to me.

Howard Ball

For many years, I listened to message after message on how I should be kind to other people, help meet their needs, and love them. But I didn't have the power to be that kind of person. I attended church on Sunday, even taught a Sunday school class, but I had no concept of a personal God.

Sometimes people I contacted in sales work would ask things like, "Are you saved?"

But I would just laugh at them. "Saved? I didn't even know I was in trouble."

I'm sure now that they were trying to communicate God's love to me, but they didn't know how.

One day the wife of a friend invited Barbara to a Bible class. Barbara did everything she could to get out of it, but finally ran out of excuses. So she asked me to go with her. I had no desire to sit with a bunch of peculiar people while they talked about a book that had never made sense to me. Besides, the class conflicted with my night out at the club with my buddies.

But I reluctantly went, sat down, crossed my arms, and leaned back with an attitude. "Well, you got me here. Now amaze me." And was I amazed! I couldn't believe what the person who led the

Bible study did. She stood before the group and said, "I don't want you to take my word for anything, unless you find it substantiated in the Bible." That was refreshing. I hadn't planned on taking anything seriously anyway.

Then the leader read from John 1. For the first time, I considered the fact that either the Bible is telling the truth when it says Jesus is God or it is lying. That night after class, the friend whose wife had invited Barbara asked me about my impressions of the study.

"Look, Jim," I scowled, "I've been around the block at least twice and there's no free lunch. So don't give me the idea, 'Here's God on a platter. All you've got to do is ask and you can have Him.' I don't buy it. You get out of life exactly what you put into it. There's a catch in this somewhere."

Three weeks later, as I sat at my office desk, a question suddenly popped into my mind: *What about Christ? Could what I heard at that Bible study be true?* I shrugged off the thought and got busy. But the question persisted. Finally, I threw down my pen in disgust and decided not to play games with religion. As I reflected on what I had heard at the Bible study, I tried to reason it out. But I couldn't handle it. It wouldn't fit. Suddenly, the light went on. I'd had thirty years of broken New Year's resolutions to prove that I knew what I should be, but lacked the power to be. I prayed, "Okay, Lord, if You're in this life-changing business, here's one. Have at it."

And that day, He began to "have at it." I began reading the Bible with an amazing hunger and understanding. Life took on new meaning and purpose. As the days passed, I began loving people I hadn't even liked before.

One day I came across Galatians 5:22,23: "The fruit of the Spirit is love, joy, peace, patience, kindness, goodness, faithfulness, gentleness, and self-control." I leaned back in my chair and laughed, realizing that all of my unkept New Year's resolutions were related to these qualities. Now I was experiencing them but I wasn't "doing it" myself; Christ was producing them in my life.

I also realized that everyone I meet is God-hungry just like I was, and most probably don't understand that only God can satisfy their need. I determined to invest my life in helping others hear the gospel because it's the key that unlocks everything else.

Through the years, Barbara and I have seen literally thousands of people respond to the "good news" shared in our home and in the homes of others in our country and around the world.

People relax and give "favorable attention" in a home setting more readily than anywhere else. What a fulfilling joy it is to see God's power transform others as we make ourselves available for His use.

Helen Headley

In September 1967, a friend asked if I would co-host an evangelistic coffee in October. She was arranging a week-long series of coffees, one each morning. A group of Christian businessmen and their wives were going to visit our city and the women wanted places to speak on "The Reality of Christ in Your Life."

When I agreed to co-host the event, my friend assigned me to Thursday morning. Hanging up the telephone, I wondered, *Why did I say I'd do that? I need one more thing to do like I need a hole in my head!*

At that time, I was thirty-something and my husband and I had three children, ages 12, 9, and 5. My husband and I were active in our church. In addition, we had moved into our dream home just two years before, and fixing it up still occupied a lot of my time. Civic activities claimed more time.

But when the week of the coffees arrived, I could hardly wait for the first one. I encouraged women to go, although I didn't really know why.

Barbara Ball, the scheduled speaker, shared about her life years ago, and I was stunned. Her life sounded so much like mine—so full, but so empty. With all I had, I still felt a void that nothing could fill. Even in a crowded room, I felt lonely. Something was missing.

I never dreamed that my problem was spiritual. After all, weren't we active in our church? I did try hard to do all the right things. I believed that Jesus died for me, and I had made a public profession of faith in Christ during my junior high years.

But that day, Barbara shared the *Four Spiritual Laws,* a simple presentation of the gospel. When she got to Law Four, she pointed out that it is not enough to believe in Christ, but that we also must receive Him into our lives. Then she led us in prayer.

Silently, I asked the Lord to come into my life and make me what He wanted me to be. Then I remember Barbara saying, "If you asked Jesus into your life, where is He now?"

I knew that He was in my life. No bells sounded; no emotional experience rocked me. But in the following days, I noticed that the void was gone. I had an inner peace that I had never experienced before.

These twenty-plus years since then have been a time of learning to die to myself and live for Him. I have encountered many trials and difficulties, but His grace and peace have always been more than enough!

Gail Frank

I had been living a self-centered life, working hard at my career, and taking care of my husband's and my own wants and needs. We assumed that one day we would be parents, but an unexpected surgery removed the possibility of a pregnancy. We dealt with our problems the best way we could, but we really didn't know how to look to God for comfort. So our lives just sort of moved along . . .

Then in 1985, my life took a different path. I was invited to a home to hear about one person's discovery of fulfillment in life (or so the invitation read). I chose not to attend, but was invited to the Bible study that followed. I decided to go to that.

During those weekly meetings, I heard about a personal relationship with Jesus Christ. As I worked through the lesson material, I assured myself that I had that relationship. After all, I'd grown up in the church, and I knew who God was and the purpose for Jesus' death. Rose Sutherland, a friend in the study, later told me that she was sure each session would be my last because I had such an intense look on my face and didn't say anything.

Actually, I was fully absorbed in the discussion. Each night following the study, I would lay in bed next to my husband and share with him the things I had heard. He thought I should continue attending.

I soon found myself in a chain of life-sharing events. Several weeks later, someone again invited me to a home where a woman gave her personal testimony. Rose presented the *Four Spiritual Laws,* and that night I asked Jesus Christ to come into my life. I was born again! I was not fully aware of the extent of the commitment I made, but I did have the assurance that I would spend eternity in heaven.

The woman who shared her testimony that night had invited Christ into her life at a previous outreach held at another woman's home. God used Rose to lead me to Christ that evening, and since then, my husband has also received Christ. Now I have the privilege of sharing my testimony in homes opened by other ladies who want their friends and neighbors to know the love of Christ, too. Opening your home—what a beautiful way to share the gospel in a warm, friendly, small-group setting!

Starting the Adventure

Life sharing is more fun and rewarding than you might expect. Are you ready to take the first step in this adventure? As I think of the possibility of your involvement in this home ministry, I encourage you to live as a positive witness for Jesus Christ. The words of Paul ring so true:

> Though I am far away from you my heart is with you, happy because you are getting along so well, happy because of your strong faith in Christ. And now just as you trusted Christ to save you, trust him, too, for each day's problems; live in vital union with him (Colossians 2:5,6, TLB).

I'd like to suggest four ingredients that will help make your ministry fruitful:

First, *trust Jesus to do what He promises.* He said, "All authority in heaven and on earth has been given to me" (Matthew 28:18), and, "You may ask me for anything in my name, and I will do it"

(John 14:14). With these promises, we can step out in faith and share our testimony with others.

Second, *obey Jesus.* He said, "If you love me, you will obey what I command" (John 14:15). Obedience is active proof that we are relying on His promises.

Third, *remain in Jesus.* He said, "I am the vine; you are the branches. If a man remains in me and I in him, he will bear much fruit; apart from me you can do nothing" (John 15:5). To remain in Jesus means to live under the control and power of the Holy Spirit, with no unconfessed sin.

Fourth, *receive training* (2 Timothy 3:14–17). Learn how to share your faith more effectively. In later chapters, we will give you practical help in giving your testimony and in using the *Four Spiritual Laws.* We will also provide material to help you demonstrate a life-sharing event.

Trusting, obeying, remaining in Jesus, and receiving training. I challenge you to follow this simple formula to see the impact this ministry will have in your life as well as in the lives of your friends, neighbors, coworkers, loved ones, and others in your sphere of influence. See what God will do through you—and through your home!

Now that we've laid the groundwork, we're ready to start!

CHAPTER 5

Developing a Neighborhood Ministry

Barbara

VONETTE AND I have some delightful friends, Norm and
Becky Wretland, who have developed a life-sharing ministry
with couples. But the Wretlands didn't start out as dynamic
witnesses. I'd like you to hear their story in Becky's words:

Becky

Norm and I moved into our first house in 1969. It was located in
a California city on a cul-de-sac lined with jacaranda trees. For three
years we visited with our neighbors across our fences and in our
front yards, we participated in block parties, and we exchanged
stories about our kids and their teachers. But never once did we
mention the name of Jesus to any of them.

Active in our church, we considered ourselves good Christians.
We knew we were to witness for Christ, but we didn't know how
to go about it, especially with our neighbors.

One night, Norm and I had a heated argument in our front
yard over that very issue. But we closed our argument in prayer,
asking God to show us what to do. That same week, a friend invited
us to a weekend training seminar on—would you believe it—wit-

nessing! The friend even offered to babysit our children for the whole weekend. That was an offer we couldn't pass up, and we had a strange feeling that God was answering our prayer.

That weekend changed our lives! Armed with information on how to use the *Four Spiritual Laws* booklet, we had found the confidence we needed to reach out to our neighbors.

Twenty-Three Years of Miracles

From that day on, we began to share Christ with our neighbors. During the next twenty-three years, we saw many miracles. Not only were the lives of our two daughters greatly affected, but many neighbors received Christ, and now their children and grandchildren are coming to know Jesus as well.

Before long I invited Marlis to a women's coffee, assuming that she was already a Christian. However, she received Christ that day, but didn't tell me until two days later. I was surprised and ecstatic! Then she helped us plan a Christmas party for about twenty-five neighbors. We were too timid to ask an outside speaker to give a testimony, so at the last minute Norm agreed to speak. He began by asking people to tell about their Christmas memories or family traditions, then he shared some of his traditions and wove in his testimony.

Marlis couldn't contain herself. She blurted out, "I've just become a Christian a few weeks ago," shocking her husband, who had been a closet Christian for years.

Soon Marlis and I began a women's neighborhood Bible study. Before long, we saw two women receive Christ as their Savior. When Norm and I sold our home and moved to another state, the couple who purchased our house became Christians after attending the Bible study for only two weeks! The woman said she knew that God had led her to our neighborhood.

We made our new home in Texas, and after three weeks, we planned to open our home so that we could meet our neighbors. About twenty-five people walked through our door that Sunday afternoon, and within the next three years, ten of them became Christians.

We began holding evangelistic Christmas parties, women's Valentine coffees, and couples' pool parties. We also started a ladies' Bible study that continued for eight years, a couples' neighborhood Bible study, and a morning men's Bible study. Those Bible studies became the talk of the neighborhood.

Snowball Evangelism

During the years we lived in that area, through neighbor reaching neighbor, more than sixty people began a relationship with Jesus. I entitle our story "Snowball Evangelism" because of the tremendous effect neighborhood evangelism has. Once that ball starts rolling, it just gets bigger and bigger. Here are a few examples:

Mary Pat came to a Valentine's coffee because she received an attractive red-and-white invitation. Afraid to go alone, she invited her next-door neighbor to come along. Five days after the coffee, Mary Pat and Bruno, her huge St. Bernard, stood at my door. Tears ran down her cheeks, but she smiled and said, "Becky, I went into my bathroom yesterday afternoon to think, and I asked Christ to come into my heart and be my Savior. I have such peace and excitement now, I just had to walk down and tell you." I embraced her, while Bruno tried to get into our circle of love.

The snowball had started rolling. Mary Pat went on to become a Bible study leader. Today her husband is the treasurer of the church that began in our neighborhood as a result of these parties and Bible studies. Recently, we received a letter from her teenage son regarding his mission trip to Guatemala this summer...

Gena and Jim, who were new Christians, invited their backyard neighbors, Sharon and Dennis, to our first Christmas party. Dennis accepted Christ that night and Sharon renewed her commitment. Then Sharon invited Hilde, who was on her bowling team, to a ladies' Bible study. Hilde received Christ not long after, so Dennis and Sharon invited Hilde and her husband, Dwight, to a couples' pool party. Dwight accepted Christ that night.

Then Hilde told her back-alley neighbor, Jeanne, about how she had just become a Christian, and Jeanne began attending the Bible study with her. I had the privilege of sharing the *Four*

Spiritual Laws with Jeanne. Two days later, she asked me to come to her home. "Today, for the first time," she said, "I know I have eternal life." She had received Christ just that afternoon.

For several months, Jeanne's husband, Jerry, made fun of her new faith. Finally he agreed to attend our second neighborhood Christmas party. Four of the couples who had received Christ during that year gave short testimonies. Jerry was impressed with their courage and sincerity, and two months later he received Christ. Today he is an elder in a local church. His six children are now Christians and his grandchildren are finding the Lord.

Jerry and Jeanne were friends with Sue and Jerry who lived on the next street. Jerry and Jeanne invited them to hear a talk on evolution versus creation. That was a hot topic for Sue and Jerry, and he asked many questions. Soon after that evening, he received Christ. Sue began attending the ladies' Bible study, and she became a Christian, too. That was six years ago. Three years later, she died of cancer—but not without Christ! . . .

We moved from Texas to Colorado five years ago. Since then, we've helped train people in our church in Denver in evangelistic entertaining and have seen more than a hundred Christmas parties take place. A neighborhood coffee and Bible study have sprung up in our neighborhood. Two women recently received Christ and we have invited their husbands to an evangelistic Passover Seder dinner on Good Friday.

God continues His work, and He allows us the privilege of being a part of it. We find our greatest joy in seeing a new Christian born and watching him or her grow up in Christ.

Snowball evangelism is spiritual multiplication. God doesn't just enlarge our ministry through simple addition where we witness to one person, then to another. Instead, He multiplies our efforts. We lead someone to the Lord, and they in turn introduce their friends to Jesus, and then those new Christians begin winning others to Christ. Soon the efforts have multiplied far beyond any of our own spheres of influence.

Barbara

Does Becky's story thrill you as much as it does us? Or do you feel a little overwhelmed? As you'll learn in this book, developing a ministry in your neighborhood isn't difficult. It takes only some personal preparation and a reasonable amount of bridge-building.

Preparing Yourself

No matter what we decide to do, we have to prepare for it. Before beginning a trip, we plan the route, pack our belongings, and check the car. It's no less important to prepare spiritually for ministry. One of the best ways I've found to remain encouraged, activated, and trusting God is to maintain my fellowship with Him. In an earlier chapter, Vonette shared the concept of Spiritual Breathing. What a gift from a grace-filled God! And I know it works—I've experienced it often through the years.

While preparing a holiday meal one New Year's Eve, I discovered that my oven wouldn't work. Adding to my annoyance, the dishwasher started leaking and two faucets began dripping. And it was a holiday—I couldn't call a serviceman. How would I prepare hot dishes to bring to a New Year's Eve celebration at Bill and Vonette's home? Was I upset!

Graciously, Vonette said I could bring my uncooked food to her house and use her oven. When I arrived early, Bill cheerfully asked, "Barbara, are you looking forward to the new year?"

With my arms full, I muttered, "If it's like today, I don't think so."

"What's wrong?"

I told him the miseries of my day. And he responded, "The Bible says to give thanks in everything. Have you given thanks?"

I immediately realized that my heart was planted right in the middle of my circumstances rather than in the middle of God's love. So, breathing spiritually, I began to give thanks. You can guess what happened. I enjoyed the evening and actually looked forward to the new year.

Let me suggest three mental approaches that will help you prepare yourself for an effective, fulfilling ministry.

Be Ready

The apostle Paul tells us in 2 Timothy 4:2, "Preach the Word of God urgently at all times, whenever you get the chance, in season and out, when it is convenient and when it is not" (TLB). Breathing spiritually is part of staying prepared. However, we must also develop a positive attitude. We must be ready for anything. Just as a sprinter crouches in position for a fast break, we need to position ourselves to share the gospel with everyone who will listen. We cannot wait until we have a party to share our faith.

Part of continuing readiness is consistent prayer for our neighbors. When we bring them before the Lord, our spiritual vision stays clear. When you pray for them, ask God to prepare their hearts for your witness.

For the next part of readiness, make yourself available. Being ready "in season and out" means taking the time to stop and talk to your neighbors when you see them, or to help them fix their lawn mower or bake them brownies. When they see your openness with them, they will be more open to you and what you have to say about God.

Be Flexible

Another way we can prepare ourselves is by being flexible. As with any other activity we attempt, lots of things can go wrong. People do things we don't expect, our plans don't fall into place like we would like, and unexpected last-minute crises arise. We may miss great opportunities for ministry if we cannot change our plans on short notice.

This last Christmas, Howard and I were thrilled to have our daughter Robbyn, grandson Tobin, and my mother home for the holidays. It's always a treat to be with Robbyn; she's an excellent gourmet cook.

We invited company over one night—some good friends whose house guest was Luci Swindoll, sister of the renowned Bible teacher Charles Swindoll. We wanted the dinner to be informal, so Robbyn came up with a new pasta recipe, caesar salad, grilled sausages, and a special ice cream parfait dessert.

When we greeted our guests, we immediately felt as though we had always known Luci. As we began our evening relaxing over appetizers, some Christmas carolers came by. They brought a special glow to our hearts, and when they left, we resettled into our chairs. Robbyn gently reminded Howard and me, "Mom, the salad, and Dad, the sausages. We're about ready to eat."

Realizing that I had forgotten the final touches on the salad, I jumped up. While I worked in the kitchen, Howard came in. "Do we have an alternative menu?" he asked sheepishly.

I turned around and saw a plate of black sausages—burnt to a crisp. *Oh, no!* I thought. *How could you have done this?*

But Robbyn saved the night. "Mom, make a lot of salad!"

We started laughing and decided that we would show our guests what they would *not* be served. As we announced dinner, we presented the burnt offerings.

Luci loved it, and our friends just had to take pictures!

Well, not everything goes right every time. When things go wrong, get up and go on! Learn to quickly develop a "Plan B." Don't wear yourself out trying to do things *so* right. When you're flexible, you can trust in the Lord and laugh at yourself!

Be Creative

Most people think they are not creative. But since God is the Creator of the universe, to say that we are not creative when we have been made in His image is unthinkable. Of course, only God can create something out of nothing. We have to begin with something. But for us to be creative simply means that we do different things, or we do the same things in different ways. While we lived in California, Howard came up with a novel idea: a casual get-together but with gourmet food. He called it Grubby Gourmet.

He planned picnics on our lawn, with a menu of fancy foods. We would set a theme, such as Mexican or Italian, and ask people to bring gourmet dishes to serve ten or more people, depending on how many we invited. The event culminated in someone sharing a testimony.

We have used this idea in a number of ways. Once we sat around the pool at the home of our dear friends Bill and Mary Frances Smith while Brad Budde, a former NFL player with the Kansas City Chiefs, shared his testimony. Brad described his father, who had also played with the Chiefs, as the ultimate example whose influence had helped Brad come to know Christ.

Another time, Bill Wenke, a lawyer who was head of the California Bar Association, gave his testimony to other lawyers and their wives at a backyard Grubby Gourmet hosted by Brian and Jeri Simpson.

Since Howard and I have many opportunities to meet people, we were able to ask Gary Smalley to come to San Bernardino when he visited his brother in southern California. Gary spoke in the home of Bill and Mary Frances Smith and then returned later to give a seminar on relationships for people who had come to our life-sharing event. Shortly after that, we started a Bible study in the home of Chris and Sue Crawford, using Gary's video, "Hidden Keys to Loving Relationships." During that evening, we had the biggest response we've ever had!

Often our creativity comes from someone else's ideas that we can copy and adapt to our own specific purpose. One night, Howard and I invited eight guests to a dinner party with a gourmet touch. I love gourmet cooking, so I indulged myself with several new recipes. Then came dessert. Our son, Bob, and his new wife, Jill, had given me this idea when we first visited them in their new apartment. I brought out dessert plates decorated with paper doilies, and with a great flourish, set a Häagen-Dazs bar on each plate, just as Bob and Jill had done. What a joy to watch those couples sitting at our table eating ice cream bars and talking about God! I didn't know evangelism could be such fun!

God wants to work uniquely in our lives to help us serve Him and others. Our creativity will grow as we learn from each other and as we are led by the Holy Spirit. We can touch people when they hurt and love them in ways that meet their needs and help them understand God's love and forgiveness. So go ahead—don't be afraid to try something new and different. Be creative.

Building Bridges

In this age of technological wonders, it is interesting how little we know about some of the simple things in life—like being a good neighbor. We can get a message around the world in a split second; we can fax a printed page across a telephone line; we can broadcast video pictures instantly around the globe. But we don't know our next-door neighbors.

Building bridges of friendship and relationship will span that gap and make it easier to reach them for the Lord Jesus Christ. Let me suggest several practical steps that can help you.

1. *Be open to your neighbors.* Earlier, I talked about being ready in season and out. Using that biblical principle, start conversations with your neighbors. When they back out of their driveways, water their lawns, or take out their trash, wave and say hi. Soon they'll be doing the same.

2. *Make a point of meeting them.* Take over homemade goodies or offer to pick up something from the store for them. If you both have young children, take your kids over to play or offer to babysit.

3. *Examine your house, making it inviting to encourage friendship.* Are your draperies open or closed? Perhaps you might put a welcome wreath on the door. Do you answer the door with a friendly smile?

4. *Go a step further and invite your neighbors over for a casual dinner or an outdoor barbecue.* When you offer hospitality first, it makes them feel wanted and important. And they will catch a glimpse of Christ's hospitable spirit. When your neighbors arrive, ask questions about their lives and interests. Ask them how they like to spend their time. Use any common interests or experiences to relate as one friend with another.

5. *As you build bridges to your neighbors, plan events for life sharing and follow-up.* Focus on Jesus Christ, and He will give you some great ideas. With your caring heart, you will want to put your love into action.

Begin Today

Friendly hospitality has helped me develop an exciting ministry. It's easy and so much fun.

Are we saying too much about how we enjoy what we are doing? Do you feel overwhelmed with so many activities? The reason I ask is that a good friend, Ney Bailey, said that she finds some preparations for a hospitality event difficult.

Ney, a sought-after speaker and author, has wonderful gifts of mercy and hospitality. She and her housemate, Mary Graham, have an open home. And when you get there, you want to stay!

One day Mary Jane Morgan, Nina Locke, Ruth Bates, and I went to an afternoon tea in their home right after they moved to Orlando. We planned to bring scones, muffins, chocolates, and cucumber sandwiches. Then we decided to make the tea a real event. The four of us "dressed up for tea." We wore 1940's style tea dresses with hats and gloves. Mary and Ney knew we were coming, but had not expected this! They greeted us with surprise, and we all had a good laugh.

We took lots of pictures. The party started at 3 p.m. and didn't end until 11 that evening. We stayed for dinner and almost spent the night!

The tea was successful because of Ney and Mary's generous hospitality. Ney then admitted that she doesn't like to cook, nor does she have the time. Guess what! You don't have to be a great cook. Today, we can get wonderful food from many different places. Ney often has pizza delivered or serves soup and sandwiches. Neither do you have to have a perfect house, table settings, or hosting skills. All you need is Christ and His love flowing through you as you reach out to others.

We encourage you to activate your gift of hospitality. In the next section of this book, we will show you how to plan, set up, and host an event. Enjoy your family, neighbors, and friends. Be involved. And discover that evangelism can be fun!

The Heart of Life Sharing

Life sharing helps us build bridges to nonbelievers for presenting the gospel in nonthreatening, easily adaptible ways. We experience the joy of hospitality as we plan, set up, and host these events.

CHAPTER 6

Making Entertaining Fun

Vonette

WHILE BILL and I continued our ministry to college students, God was working. In His timing, we were able to live in a house that was not only near the campus, but also above our financial means.

It all started when Bill was impressed of the Lord to investigate the trade or sale of a property in prestigious Bel Air, only three minutes from the center of the UCLA campus. The builder had copied a European Moorish castle, with twelve-inch-thick walls of compressed granite covered with white stucco and lots of decorative Spanish tile. It also had a red tile roof. Built in an "H" shape with two separate wings connected by the entry hall and a thirty-foot dining room, the house appeared ideal for two families and perfect for entertaining.

When Dr. Henrietta Mears, a dear friend of ours, learned of our interest in the property, God worked another miracle. She was the director of Christian Education at Hollywood Presbyterian Church. Because of her profound influence on Bill, he had received Christ as his Savior, and later she personally led me to Christ.

When she heard about the house, she became very excited and suggested that we combine households. Dr. Mears made the investment; we paid rent and shared household expenses. We often said, "She lived with us in her house." Some people were not optimistic about two women living in the same house, but for us it worked wonderfully.

In fact, we shared the Bel Air home for almost ten years. We could easily accommodate three hundred students when we pushed furniture aside and let the students sit on the floor, and we could position a speaker to be seen by three rooms of people at once.

Miss Mears loved a party! To her, being a Christian was the most positive, wonderful experience a person could have. She looked for opportunities to prove that point.

In the 1950s, Christians were generally modest and dressed conservatively, and their manner, possessions, and actions mirrored their attire. Miss Mears was loving and conservative in her biblical views but flamboyant, positive, and elaborate in her dress and her possessions. She was frugal but generous, and extravagant when she entertained. She wanted people to understand that a person did not have to give up everything to become a Christian.

Dr. Mears and I had great times together. She had so many lovely accessories that could make any occasion—a tea, dinner, or brunch—look spectacular. I delighted in planning and hosting parties with her. I learned so much from her and am doing much of what I do today because of her.

Living with her was one of God's miracles in our lives. Our house was made for spectacular parties—inside and out. It became the "Christian Hospitality Center" for southern California. We held parties ranging from small sit-down dinners to barbecues on the lawn. Many found Christ at these events. Let me tell you about one especially memorable time.

The El Dorado Cadillac

Some of my Christian friends and I wanted to reach out to two women so we planned a luncheon that would appeal to them. One of the women, a friend of mine, could be characterized as a materialist. The other, an unbeliever, had been invited by two good friends who lived in another city. To impress these worldy guests, we asked our Christian friends to wear their most showy jewelry and designer dresses and to drive their biggest cars. These items meant little to me or my friends, but they would mean a lot to our non-Christian guest.

We scheduled Ethel Barrett, the well-known storyteller, to present the gospel message. Of course, Dr. Mears added zest to the party. I asked a friend to come early. Her husband had just purchased a mauve, "swanky," custom-made El Dorado Cadillac, which she had not yet driven. She was nervous about getting behind the wheel but agreed to bring the car to the party anyway. When she arrived, I asked her to park the car right in front so the other women would see it.

At times, that luncheon looked like a scene from a movie. My worldly friend arrived fashionably late, her long, straight mink stole folded over one arm with one end touching the floor. Of course, I seated her next to the Eldorado owner. Properly impressed, my friend exclaimed in dramatic tones, "Who's mauve chariot is that parked out front?"

Everything went just as planned. Both of our special guests received Christ into their lives. My once-worldly friend realized how much more important Christ is than possessions, and later began holding weekly luncheons at which she invited her friends to listen to taped sermons of outstanding pastors.

A luncheon like this is a far cry from my old "oatmeal china," but the point is, I was learning how to use the resources I had to meet the needs of the people I knew. The apostle Paul was a strategist. He said, "I have become all things to all men so that by all possible means I might save some" (1 Corinthians 9:22). We need to be strategists, too.

The Best Meal in Los Angeles

While living with Dr. Mears, I discovered that people prefer to be entertained in your home with a home-cooked meal rather than going out to eat. I learned this lesson the hard way.

When Dr. Bill Fletcher, a friend from Oklahoma City, came to Los Angeles on business, he called to say that he had a free evening. My Bill called from his office to tell me that he had invited Dr. Fletcher to dinner. I said, "Good, we'll take him out."

Bill was silent. "It's Monday," I quickly explained. "I've been doing laundry all day. I'm tired and have nothing to serve but hamburgers."

Bill sighed. "Okay, we'll take him out."

I had forgotten that most of the fine restaurants in Los Angeles were closed on Mondays. We drove to every one we knew, found them all closed, and became more embarrassed as we drove. Finally, we ended up going to Dr. Fletcher's hotel and, at his insistence, were his guests for dinner.

As we ended the evening, Dr. Fletcher thanked us for a lovely time. But I'll never forget his gracious remark as we parted. "For your future information, I would far rather have had a hamburger seated at your table, Vonette, than to eat at any fancy restaurant in all of Los Angeles."

"The next time you come to town, we'll have you in our home for dinner," I promised.

But there was no next time. Bill Fletcher passed away a few months later. Many times since, I've reminded myself that it does not matter whether my home is fancy or plain, the food elaborate or simple. It is the hospitality that people respond to.

Sure, entertaining is work. But when we do it to serve our Lord, hospitality takes on a different meaning. During those early days of our ministry, students came to our home weekly—sometimes three or four hundred at a time! Furniture had to be moved to make room and mountains of food had to be cooked. But we were so excited because in almost every meeting, at least one person committed his or her life to Christ.

Our work on campus launched us into other ministries—forty-four of them by 1995. Outreach entertaining with a purpose had its beginning in those early days. And our Lord has blessed us with such wonderful results all these years!

Attitude and Opportunities

As the ministry of Campus Crusade began to grow in the 1950s, more staff joined our efforts. Having more experience in sharing my faith than the new staff members, I expected to graduate from kitchen duty to purely ministering to students.

But Bill pointed out that our new staff wouldn't get their training if they served in the kitchen. I agreed outwardly, but began to resent working behind the scenes. I identified with Martha in the Bible who was burdened with much serving while her sister Mary attended to the Lord. Like Martha, I felt "put upon" and my disposition probably showed it.

About this time, Bill began to teach about the person and work of the Holy Spirit. I learned that Christ didn't want me to work for Him, but He wanted to do His work in and through me by the power of His Holy Spirit. All He wanted was my availability, and He would do the rest. I began to rely on the truth of 1 Thessalonians 5:24: "The one who calls you is faithful and he will do it." I felt so liberated when I realized that *He* would control *my* circumstances and that *He* would provide the financing, wisdom, and power for me to accomplish what He asked me to do.

Seeing myself more and more as a servant of the Lord, I prepared food as unto Jesus, washed dishes for Him, and did all of my tasks because I loved Him and wanted to serve Him.

My attitude changed and I found joy in what I was doing. Entertaining was now a privilege, not an obligation. I saw in a new way that all the resources God had given me and all the opportunities I had could be used in His service.

I have since gained much experience in life sharing and have discovered that when we open ourselves to God's leading, He will guide us to needy people and show us many types of events we can host for Him.

Like Spokes in a Wheel

As Barbara and I have emphasized all along, your home is the most natural place for life sharing. You and your guests are the most comfortable there. You don't have to go somewhere else to plan or host the event. Almost everything you need is right at your fingertips. Your neighbors are close by and will feel honored that you have invited them into your home. The expense is less since you won't have to rent a room or plan a menu that must be catered. Your family can be part of your ministry. Follow-up is easier because you already have a place in which to conduct Bible studies and other follow-up activities.

None of us likes to admit that expense is a factor in ministry, but it is. One way to deal with that problem is to accept that we simply use what God has given us to the greatest benefit of others. Bill and I have been in ministry for more than forty-five years, and many times God has stretched our faith through financial concerns. But He has always provided what we need when we need it.

After one of our meetings, Bill unexpectedly invited a man to our home who had been generously supporting our ministry. He was not a Christian, and Bill wanted him to see the students who were the fruits of his investment and to challenge him to receive Christ as his Savior.

Our home was modest compared to his. When he and Bill arrived, Bill asked if I had a dessert to serve. I excused myself and went to the kitchen. Opening a cupboard door, I prayed, "Lord, what can I put together quickly that will be nice enough to serve this gentleman?"

I saw a box of gingerbread mix and thought of the applesauce and whipping cream in the refrigerator. I couldn't make coffee since we had none in the house. Would you believe I served hot gingerbread with applesauce and whipped cream along with tall glasses of milk?

The man was impressed! This was the first time in years someone had offered him something other than an alcoholic beverage. Before leaving, he asked, "Could my wife and I go to church with you this Sunday?" Delighted, Bill invited him and his wife for dinner, too.

Since finances were tight for Bill and me, I needed something inexpensive that could cook while we were at church. I decided on meatloaf. I'm sure the Lord was directing my steps because meatloaf turned out to be one of the man's favorite foods, and he hadn't eaten any for a long time. A few weeks later, they both received Christ and ultimately helped to influence many thousands for Christ.

We sometimes think that we must have "things," or that we need a lot of money to entertain. But true hospitality is sharing what is available; it is doing everything possible to make the guest feel welcome and comfortable. If what you have is dedicated to God, He will use it whether it is little or much.

Picture a wheel on a covered wagon. Your home is the hub of your ministry, but like the spokes on the wheel, your influence can radiate outward and touch many more lives. Barbara and I have given our personal testimonies and hosted events in many places besides our homes. You, too, can find opportunities in your community. Let me suggest brunches at a club, lunch-hour events at your workplace, socials at facilities that can serve many more people than your home can accommodate, special gatherings at a health club or recreation center, and picnics. The possibilities are unlimited.

A Great Idea

Shortly after Campus Crusade headquarters moved from West Los Angeles to Arrowhead Springs, California, Bill and I were invited to Anchorage, Alaska, to conduct a Lay Institute for Evangelism. A huge earthquake had recently rocked and devastated the Anchorage area. People seemed more open to the gospel, and churches in the city were united in teaching people how to share their faith.

We were busy every evening with meetings and training sessions, but our days were free. Bill suggested, "Why not schedule morning coffee times and afternoon teas for women?"

With a sense of excitement, I could see the possibilities. Twice a day, while enjoying those social events, I could share my personal experience with Christ and tell how He had changed my life.

In those days, we were still developing our procedures for effective witnessing. At the close of my testimony, I would ask the women to join me in a prayer, giving them an opportunity to receive Christ. I then asked them to write their names on a piece of paper that I handed out and to indicate with an "X" if they had prayed the prayer for the first time. Knowing who had invited Christ into their lives enabled the hosts and me to see the fruit of our efforts. Eventually, Bill and I used this approach for closing meetings in communities around the world.

Little by little, the pieces of life sharing came together. We saw the importance of getting the names of those who attended so we could follow up on their commitments and help them become established in their faith. The comments the guests wrote on the pieces of paper helped us evaluate their response and the effectiveness of our presentations. We have done this at breakfast meetings, luncheons for both men and women, and outreach dinner parties in clubs, hotels, and homes.

To help you be more effective in your life-sharing ministry, Barbara and I want you to know what has worked for us—the kinds of people we invite, the times of day that work well, and various ideas for parties and gatherings that you can host in your neighborhood.

Irresistible Invitations

Hilde Trawick of Nashville, Tennessee, planned a March tea for her neighbors. When a storm dumped piles of snow just before the event, Hilde wasn't sure anyone would come, but she decided to go ahead with her plans anyway. Thirty-five showed up in spite of the weather.

The Holy Spirit filled the house, and Hilde reported, "The women were so hungry for what our speakers had to say and identified so strongly with them that half the guests were in tears by the end of the talk." After reading through the *Four Spiritual Laws* with all the guests, Judy, one of the speakers, took two or three women to the den. Joyce, the second speaker, sat down in the living room with two others.

Long after the noon hour when the tea was supposed to end, small groups of people were still nestled in various parts of the house. Ten women received Christ, and that evening one husband did also.

All kinds of people will come to a life-sharing gathering. Some women may be available during the day, and may enjoy getting together for brunches, coffees, teas, and luncheons. If you have a morning brunch or an afternoon coffee, you may need to take into account what mothers will do with their children. Working women will need a weekend or evening event invitation.

Men also enjoy gatherings planned just for them. They like parties centered around sporting events, barbecues, and breakfasts. We have found weekends work best for those events.

Many singles appreciate coming to a home for home-cooked food. Their schedules, which may be more flexible, will depend on whether they work or are in school. Since singles like to be active, plan lively parties and meetings. Don't be afraid to invite them to events that include married couples. Pool parties, barbecues, and neighborhood get-togethers especially attract couples.

Perhaps you have never considered beginning a life-sharing ministry for youth and children. Young people are attracted to homes that offer acceptance and love. In a later chapter, we will show you how to reach out to teens in your neighborhood or in the junior or senior high school near your home. Elementary-age youngsters enjoy parties, and their hearts are open to the gospel. A neighborhood children's club will produce much fruit. And what a joy it will be to follow up these little ones after they receive Christ as their Savior.

A Chart for Planning

Perhaps you're thinking, *I've never hosted an event. How do I start? What do I do when my guests arrive?* Let me give you some suggestions that you may find helpful.

Much of the success of an evangelistic event comes from proper planning. Although you must be flexible to allow for changes, knowing what you intend to do and when will make your guests feel more secure. The following chart provides some guidelines as you schedule your event.

Before you begin planning, make a similar chart listing specific tasks for each helper participating in your meeting. We have included a blank chart in the Resources section at the end of the book. Pencil in your plans, readjusting the chart as necessary. As you become more familiar with hosting life-sharing gatherings, you may want to change your chart or headings to fit your events.

WHAT	WHEN	HOW
1. Pray and start planning.	At least four weeks before your event, although short notice or spur-of-the-moment gatherings can also be effective	Prayer is the most important element in planning and hosting a party. Pray before you begin. Ask those you would like to help and set up times to pray with them. Seek God's direction, blessing, and power. When you know what He wants you to do, begin creating a schedule and listing supplies you will need.
2. Select your speaker.	At the beginning stages of planning	If you desire a speaker to present a testimony, ask that person well in advance. That will give your speaker time to prepare and will help you plan the gathering around his or her topic.
3. Train your helpers.	During the planning stage	Training may include tips for hosts and hostesses, and sessions on how to lead a person to Christ, how to prepare and give a personal testimony, and how to do follow-up. The chapter on hosting a demonstration meeting gives excellent material on how to train others in life sharing.
4. Plan your follow-up.	During the planning stage	Plan for a Bible study or one-to-one appointment, and gather any needed materials.

WHAT	WHEN	HOW
5. Send out invitations.	Written invitations two or three weeks in advance; oral invitations one week in advance	Use both written and oral invitations for your meeting. Written invitations help your guests confirm the time. An oral invitation given after the written one will serve as a reminder and encourage that person to attend.
6. Set up the event.	Begin several hours before your guests are due to arrive.	Allow plenty of time for preparations on the day of your meeting. You will need to get food ready, arrange the room, gather materials, and attend to many other details. Avoid making your event a last-minute rush, which invites catastrophe.
7. Host the event.	1½ to 2 hours, depending on your gathering	This, of course, is where all your work comes together. Be prepared to change details of your plans as problems arise. Focus your attention on your guests rather than on food preparation or other work.
8. Help guests come to know Christ.	After the speaker concludes	This is what the entire event is all about. With planning and help from other Christians, you can counsel everyone who responds to an invitation to receive Christ.
9. Follow-up those who respond.	As soon as possible after the event	Encourage those who respond to the invitation to receive Christ to attend follow-up sessions.
10. Evaluate your event.	Within two or three days	Many people shy away from evaluation because they think it means criticism. But evaluation serves a much different purpose. Through prayer and discussion, you can decide how better to meet the needs of your guests at future events.

Examples of Attractive Events

The suggestions below will give you ideas for certain events, though we're sure you can come up with creative ideas of your own. In the following chapters, you will learn how to plan, set up, and host events, including the types of events listed here.

Coffees

This informal gathering may be held in the morning, afternoon, or evening. The menu is usually light, such as snacks or small sandwiches with the coffee. Ask a speaker to present the gospel through a personal testimony.

Grubby Gourmet

Invite your guests for a planned potluck, featuring gourmet food and grubby (casual) dress. Ask a special guest to share a personal testimony.

Barbecues

This event can be held in a backyard or a park. Plan food that can be cooked on a grill and eaten outdoors. After the meal, ask someone to share a personal testimony. Then close with games such as backyard volleyball or croquet.

Jazzercize

While you're exercising at your neighborhood health club, introduce yourself to other club members and build friendships. Plan a coffee or other event for these friends and ask an exercise expert who is a Christian to share his or her faith.

Video Presentation

Invite friends to view an evangelistic video such as *A Man Without Equal*. After the video, ask someone to give their personal testimony. Wrap up the event with food and conversation. Chapter 17 has specific information on how to host this kind of meeting.

Children's Events

If you have children in your neighborhood, host children's parties and clubs in your home. Serve simple snacks and tell a Bible story. See Chapter 14 for further help on how to hold these gatherings.

Youth Happenings

Do you have teenagers in your neighborhood or a junior or senior high school near your home? Plan an evangelistic party for teens. Provide lots of food, a lively game, and ask your Christian young people to help host the party. See Chapter 15.

Sporting Events

Whether the men and women you know like to attend sporting events, watch games on television, or play sports themselves, plan an evangelistic party around their interests. Together, attend a basketball game, play golf, or enjoy another activity. Meet back at your house afterward for refreshments. During games such as the Super Bowl or Monday night football, invite friends to your home to watch. Arrange for a speaker to give a testimony with a sports theme.

Luncheons

Luncheons can range from a casual meal to a more formal event. Some luncheons could include: pot-lucks, salad buffet, prepared deli trays, sandwiches, and even catered meals. Plan your meeting at a home, neighborhood clubhouse, restaurant, community hall, or other public facility. Send invitations and ask a special speaker to share his or her faith. You may want to form a luncheon group with other Christian friends and host monthly events to reach others for Christ.

Craft or Other Specialty Events

Invite your non-Christian friends to a sewing or needlework class or a craft-making session. During the refreshments afterward, ask a speaker to present a talk on a topic such as "The Reality of Christ in a Woman's World." These kinds of events work well around holidays or with people who have creative hobbies or interests.

Christmas Coffees

Take advantage of the Christmas season when many people are thinking about God. Your Christmas decorations are already up, and you probably have holiday baking plans, too. Invite neighbors and friends to share about their own holiday traditions and to hear a talk on the real meaning of Christmas. Chapter 16 contains specific ideas on how to host Christmas gatherings.

Brunches

Midmorning is an enjoyable time to host an event, especially around Easter. Serve a breakfast buffet or a light lunch. During an Easter brunch, arrange for a speaker to tell why Christ's resurrection means so much to us today. Saturday mornings are a good time for couples' events.

Valentine's Day Party

This is a great couples' event. Serve an appetizer buffet with beverage. Invite couples to share what Christ's love means to them.

Large Gatherings

You may find opportunities to host an event that is too large to accommodate in a home. Rent a meeting room in a clubhouse, local hotel, or restaurant. Arrange for a catered meal to which you invite your friends who would enjoy a more formal setting in which to hear an interesting speaker. We have included information on how to plan such an event in Chapter 13.

Caroling Party

Invite your neighbors to meet at your house, then go caroling to homes in the area. Afterward, provide hot chocolate and other snacks at your home and ask someone to tell how Christ brings joy into our lives.

Progressive Dinner

With other Christian couples, plan an evening where your group travels from house to house, eating different courses of a meal at each place. Begin with an appetizer, then include as many courses as you want. At one home, have the guests sit down for the main course. At the home with the dessert, arrange to have a speaker illustrate the importance of Christ in a marriage relationship.

Chili Cook-off

Invite couples to cook their best chili recipes and bring the food to your home. Provide extras such as bread, beverages, and dessert. Ask someone to judge the chili before you all eat. Afterward, give out prizes, and have someone share how knowing Christ means you're always in first place.

Tailgate Party

Plan this kind of event as a going-away gathering or just as a good time for neighbors to get together to build friendships. Set up a portable barbecue, back a pick-up or van into your driveway, decorate the inside with potted flowers, and let your guests order their food from the party van. When you invite your guests, ask them to bring their own lawn chairs. After the food has been eaten, ask a speaker to talk about how we are one in Christ.

Pool Party

Even guests who prefer not to get wet will enjoy cooling off beside a backyard pool. Begin with a time for swimming or games, then serve refreshments and introduce the speaker who will tell how Christ gives living water.

Color Demonstration

This special outreach can have a theme such as "Beauty Within and Beauty Without." Ask a friend who is trained in helping people choose colors for their wardrobe or someone who has a background in make-up applications to give a demonstration. Then close with a time of sharing that when we commit ourselves to Christ, our true beauty comes from within. He brings a radiance into our lives that will never fade.

Independence Day Gathering

Plan a neighborhood brunch with a Fourth of July theme. Place a notice on each family's door announcing that you are hosting a party with a parade. One side of the street could bring fruit and the other coffee cake. Ask the children to decorate their bicycles and wagons, and prepare a short program to put on for the adults. Watch the children's parade and program, then enjoy the brunch. As a group, you could sing patriotic songs just before the speaker gives a talk.

Block Rummage Sale

Planning this event helps neighbors get to know each other. To attract a lot of customers, advertise your event as a block sale in the newspapers. Each family is responsible for their own set-up and sale. But before customers arrive, encourage neighbors to visit each family's home to see what they have displayed. When the sale is over, meet for a potluck and have someone give a short talk.

Easter Events

Easter is an opportune time to hold an evangelistic brunch. You can serve an array of Easter breads, followed by a message on "Jesus Is the Bread of Life." Other effective Easter themes are "Easter Is More Than Bunnies and Eggs" and "Easter Traditions From Around the World." Include the Christian Easter story with a personal testimony and a clear presentation of the gospel.

Use these suggestions to plan your own event. Tailor the topic of the talk to the event and the experiences that the speaker has to share with your group. Once you have completed the planning, it will soon be time to set up for your gathering. Our next chapter shows you just how easy it can be to make your arrangements for an exciting time.

**Included in the Resources for
Effective Life Sharing**

❧ Planning Schedule

CHAPTER 7

Setting Up
the Event

Barbara

ONE DAY MY friend Ginny asked me if I would speak at an
evening coffee. The women in her Bible study wanted to
introduce their friends and families to Christ. I eagerly said yes.

When I arrived the evening of the coffee, the home looked
beautiful. I was welcomed warmly at the door and directed to the
name-tag table. I noticed another table set with mouth-watering
desserts, many of them chocolate. I am careful to eat a healthy diet,
but I do enjoy relaxing my diet on special occasions, so I looked
forward to dessert time.

Then a new friend, Linda, came in with seven guests—from
Russia! I was delighted to meet them. When Linda casually
mentioned that one of the women, Olga, would translate for the
others, I was stunned, and my head began spinning. *Should I cut
my talk short to give time for the translator? How will what I say sound
to someone from another culture?*

In the living room, the chairs were all turned to face me. As
someone introduced me, Olga translated the introduction. *I don't
think this is going to go well,* I thought. But then I remembered that

75

my message was the gospel of Christ. I claimed 1 Thessalonians 5:24, which says, "The one who calls you is faithful and he will do it." God would do His work through me—no matter how I felt.

I gave my testimony and a practical marriage illustration of how Howard and I learned a valuable lesson in forgiveness. Then I shared the *Four Spiritual Laws.* When I finished reading through the booklet, I gave the women an opportunity to receive Christ and to indicate their decision by writing an "X" on a 3×5 card, along with their name and address.

When I read the cards later, I saw that five women had marked an "X" beside their name. Olga also told me that the marriage illustration I had given was very helpful to the Russian women. I rejoiced that God had been in control, in spite of my feelings.

Now that you have planned your event, perhaps you too sense some uneasiness about your ability to handle an event. Relax! Learning how to use your home to introduce others to Jesus is a process. When God is in control, you don't have to be perfect or experienced. If you feel led by the Lord to host a life-sharing event, the Holy Spirit will guide you through the details. Vonette and I want to share some practical suggestions for setting it up. We have included a "Planning Schedule" and a "Hostess Checklist" in the Resources.

Before You Begin

Your most important decision will be to let God be God and to give Him His rightful place in your plans. Through His gracious control, His life will flow through you to others—regardless of whether the details work out exactly as you envisioned.

Colossians 4:5,6 has helped me through the planning stage of many life-sharing events:

> Behave yourselves wisely—living prudently and with discretion—in your relations with those of the outside world (the non-Christians), making the very most of the time *and* seizing (buying up) the opportunity. Let your speech at all times be gracious (pleasant and winsome), seasoned [as it

were] with salt, [so that you may never be at a loss] to know how you ought to answer any one [who puts a question to you] (Amplified).

This verse contains the basic principles for planning and hosting an event:

- ❧ Let God control your life (behave wisely).
- ❧ Don't procrastinate (make the most of your time).
- ❧ Be clear and bold, but tactful and loving (season your speech with graciousness).

Keeping this verse in my heart as I plan reminds me to make God my first priority—and the reason for my joy in serving.

Places, Plans—and People

Vonette and I have already mentioned how vital it is to consider people more important than plans. In setting up an event, it's easy to become frazzled and overly concerned with details, losing the primary focus in life sharing. I admit it—I'm guilty of this, too. I love seeing to the details, making everything look nice, fussing over the food, and studying to give a talk. That's why I'm tempted to make my plans the center of my attention.

Recently, Howard and I moved into a new home. One afternoon, I sat by the window to prepare for a message on marriage relationships. As I looked out on the back yard, I felt grateful for the beautiful greenery and the bright flowers.

Then I noticed the furniture on the patio. Howard had set extra chairs on the patio, and suddenly I became aware of how cluttered it looked. I put down my studies and went outside, then picked up the chairs and arranged them in the yard.

About that time, Howard came out of his office. "Barbara, that's not good for the chairs. I put them on the patio because the humidity and the mildew will be worse when they're on the grass."

"Do whatever you want!" I shot back and marched into the house.

Standing at the kitchen window, I watched him place the chairs back on the patio. "I can't believe this!" I muttered.

He didn't see or hear my anger, but he did notice my attitude as I sauntered past him in the hall a few minutes later.

When I sat down to continue my message on marriage, I couldn't think. I felt empty. Then the Holy Spirit began convicting me of my bad attitude. Here I was, planning to tell others how to serve your spouse in the Lord, and demanding my way at the same time—just so the details would be the way I liked them!

I confessed my wrongdoing to the Lord, and He gave me strength to walk into Howard's office and say, "I'm sorry." He came toward me before I could get the words out and asked me to forgive him for his insensitivity. Then I asked his forgiveness. We hugged each other and went back to our separate tasks.

Later, I shared that incident during my talk to a group of women—and we all laughed! I thought I was the only one who got so caught up in having everything "right," but now I realize that this sin is common.

First John 2:1 records, "I write this to you so that you will not sin. But if anybody does sin, we have one who speaks to the Father in our defense." Confession brings joy; submission to the Lord brings laughter. When I laugh at my mistakes and failings, I find lightness and healing. After all, laughter is jogging on the inside. It creates a healthy attitude. So I do lots of it.

Another temptation I face when things go wrong is frustration. But I've found that giving thanks to God in all circumstances (1 Thessalonians 5:18) helps me overcome that sin.

I treasure one example of how this works. When our son Bob was in elementary school, I usually gave him a snack after he got home. One day, he took his cookies and milk and sat at the counter, watching while I put away the groceries.

When I opened the refrigerator door, the side bar broke and mustard, jelly, catsup, and other bottles tumbled onto the floor—and broke! The mess began spreading all over my kitchen floor.

I'm sure you know what my normal reaction would have been—disgruntled impatience. Instead, I looked at Bob and asked, "Did you know that the Bible says to give thanks in everything?"

He muttered, "Uh-uh."

"I'm giving thanks right now for this mess and the good attitude God will give me in cleaning it up!"

Bob watched in amazement as I scrubbed up the mess. And I felt lifted up and pure instead of frustrated and angry!

Later, as Bob and a friend passed by, I overheard him say, "My mom was really great today." Then he related the incident. But better than that, at the dinner table, he announced, "Dad, I was very proud of mom today. She was really walking in the Spirit!"

Thanks be to God! When we walk in the Spirit with joy and thanksgiving, He turns all of our frustration and anger into laughter and peace. He helps me put the details into their rightful place.

Thorough Planning

What have you planned lately that turned out good even though you didn't put much time and effort into preparation? Those circumstances happen once in a while. But normally, we get out of an event just about what we put into it. If this is your first time to host a coffee, brunch, couples' party, or other event, give yourself the edge by planning thoroughly. The following steps will help.

1. Plan Early

As humans, we tend to put off until tomorrow things that need to be done today. That's why I advise starting your plans early. Those who regularly host dinners, coffees, or brunches may already know how much time to allot for planning. Each of us has our own way of preparing and hosting an outreach. Some people love to work out all the details. Others just want to "get out there and do it." But good planning is vital to a successful event. Allow four weeks for preparations. That eliminates the temptation to rush essential steps such as prayer. Emphasizing prayer and waiting on God for direction means giving yourself ample time to talk to Him.

2. Ask Others to Help You

Both men and women have a hard time asking others for help. Perhaps this stems from pride or from an insecurity over our own effectiveness in an evangelistic social event. But some of the best times I've had with Christian friends were during prayer and planning for an outreach. In the process, I have developed closer friendships and discovered more about the friends I thought I knew so well.

The old adage is true—many hands make light work. Asking Christian friends to help brings many advantages. They can help invite your guests and can suggest friends who might attend. They can help bring or prepare the refreshments and serve as co-hosts on the day of the event. They also can encourage you when you get discouraged or suggest ways to make your event better. Ask them early to give them the necessary time to prepare, too.

3. Select a Place and a Date

The location and size of the home you use will have some bearing on your other decisions, such as what type of event to have. If you have a small home, you may prefer to host a coffee or brunch rather than a sit-down meal. If someone offers a home with a pool, you may want to have a barbecue for couples. The size of the home will also determine how many guests you should invite. And that will affect the refreshments and how you will arrange other details. Once you have decided where to hold your party and the type of gathering, set a date and time that is convenient for the host or hostess and for others in your planning group.

4. Ask Someone to Be the Guest Speaker

Don't let this frighten you. You aren't planning an event at the White House. Instead, you want to create a casual, warm atmosphere for your guests. Your speaker may give his or her personal testimony and perhaps a short message on a topic of interest to those you've invited. The speaker can be someone from your church or a Christian friend outside your church, or you may decide to do this yourself. In the Special Events section, we have included ideas for a video presentation that doesn't require a speaker.

Let me suggest some topics your speaker can use:

* The Reality of Christianity in a Woman's/Man's/Couples' World

- The True Meaning of Christmas
- It Takes Two to Tango (couples topic)
- Easter Joy
- A Neighborhood That Parties Together Stays Together
- Spring Fling (tailgate party)
- How Do You Spell Relief? A Biblical Perspective on Handling Stress and Anxiety

Make sure your speaker understands his or her role in the event. Inform the speaker about your expected guests: their ages, how they might dress, their interests and their families, and any other pertinent information that will help your speaker prepare.

Ask the speaker to prepare a personal testimony from the worksheet provided in the Resources. Limit the speaker to thirty minutes if you plan to present the *Four Spiritual Laws* or forty-five minutes if he or she will go through the booklet. In the Resources, you will find material on how to present the *Four Spiritual Laws*. Ask everyone in your planning group to study this presentation until you all feel comfortable presenting the booklet to a non-Christian. Decide whether you or the speaker will close in prayer. Also discuss plans for counseling guests who have spiritual needs.

Then pray together, assuring the person that you will continue to pray for the talk. Keep in close contact to encourage and help. If your speaker is inexperienced, offer to help prepare and evaluate the talk.

The speaker should arrive at the party before the guests. Pray with the speaker and ask him or her to stand beside you as your guests come through the door so you can make introductions.

Before the program, develop a biographical sketch of your speaker to help you with your introduction. Make the sketch short enough so you can type it onto a 3×5 card for easy reference during the meeting. You might want to include information such as place of birth, education, career field, personal interests, and family information. Here are two samples of biographical sketches:

Sally Winters—Sally works at the Bank of Montreal in Los Angeles. She graduated from the Rim of the World High

School and attended California State University in San Bernardino. She enjoys hiking, reading, and attending Dodger games. In her position as a loan officer, she sees people who have many kinds of financial difficulties. Today, she's going to help us see money management from a new perspective: "Finding a Christian Blueprint for Spending and Saving."

Jim Smith—Jim was born in the small farming community of Mars, Pennsylvania. He attended Michigan State University and graduated with a degree in Agricultural Economics. For the past ten years, he has been employed by the State Agricultural Department. He and his wife, Susan, enjoy many outdoor sports, including swimming and tennis. They have two boys in elementary school. Today, Jim is going to tell us how to get the most out of a backyard garden and how gardening illustrates our relationship with Jesus Christ.

5. Send Invitations

When you are praying with those who have agreed to co-host an event, ask God to help you invite people whose hearts are open to His Word. Then list prospective guests and pray for each person individually. Include a large number of non-Christians as well as believers who can bring non-Christian friends. Don't be afraid to over-invite. We recommend asking three times as many guests as your room will hold comfortably. Last-minute interruptions often prevent people from attending.

Send written invitations to the people on your list and include an R.S.V.P. Potential guests are less likely to forget about the party if they have a written reminder. In the Resources, we have included sample invitations that you can photocopy or use as a guide.

Be honest in what you say in the invitation. Always note the speaker's topic so that no one will feel that he or she has been brought to your event under false pretenses.

While in Portland, Oregon, for a conference, I was invited to speak at an evangelistic coffee. As the guests began arriving, I was surprised that many had brought their children. Refreshments were chaotic, with dogs and children running everywhere.

As the hostess introduced me, I noticed that many of the guests had puzzled looks on their faces. I sensed their surprise to see me, so I simply told them how happy I was to be in the area and in their neighborhood and quickly sat down—much to their relief.

After everyone else had left, the hostess admitted she hadn't followed the hostess guidelines for being honest about the speaker and the topic. She was afraid her guests wouldn't come if they knew someone was going to talk to them about Christianity.

In a loving way, we discussed how her actions were deceitful. She told me she was sorry, then we prayed together. When we finished, she said, "I think the Lord wants me to apologize to my neighbors."

We went together. At each home, she told her guest how sorry she was. "I want to keep your friendship, but I wanted you to hear about Jesus Christ. Please forgive me for my deceit."

As the hostess and I went back home, I noticed how radiant she was. The joy of the Lord shone on her face. She admitted her error and had been forgiven. Now she had a unique opportunity to share God's love and forgiveness with her neighbors.

As my good friend Nina Locke says about how God works uniquely in our lives, "Isn't that just like the Lord?"

A simple way to identify your topic is to mention some form of the word Christianity or the name Jesus Christ in the invitations. Here is an example:

> Jim Banks, an accountant with Pacific Financial Services, will speak on "Biblical Principles of Money Management."

Include the date, time, place, and the telephone number of the home in which you are meeting so that the guest can reach you in case he or she can't come, needs to leave the number with a babysitter, or has trouble finding the address.

Follow up your written invitations with a telephone call. Your personal touch will help prospective guests feel more comfortable and excited about attending. You might say something like:

> I'm calling about the invitation to a coffee that you received. It's going to be at Mary Jones' home on Tuesday,

September 10 from 10 to 11:30 a.m. If you recall, the invitation mentioned that a friend will be sharing about Christian traditions in Christmas. I'm looking forward to seeing you there.

If you choose to invite guests verbally, adapt the above conversation, but be sure to include all the necessary information. Then continue to pray for those you invited. Ask God to bring people to your event and to open their hearts to the gospel.

6. Plan the Details

This is the time to finalize details of the event. What will you serve for refreshments? Write out a menu, then divide the work and food responsibilities. Will you need decorations? Does one of your friends have a talent for arranging flowers? Include her in the plans. Use as many people as possible. How about background music for the first half hour? Will you be using place cards, a centerpiece, special food items? What will you do about child care? This may be a concern for some guests. On the invitation, mention either that child care will be available or that none will be provided. This lets your guests know that the event will not interest their children. If you provide babysitting, do so in a place where the children won't disrupt your party. Make sure those who help you with your event are able to arrange for child care for their children, too.

To minimize disruptions, ask one of your helpers to sit near the telephone during the event to answer immediately if it rings. It's best to avoid having pets at your event. Many people are uncomfortable around strange animals and some may even be allergic to pet dander, so arrange to have any pets in the host's home placed where they won't disturb the guests.

Every event has late-comers. To avoid too much disruption, make a sign that says, "Welcome! Please come in and be seated," and tape it on the outside of the front door. If a guest mentions that he or she must leave early, seat them near the door.

7. Practice Conversing

If you feel uncomfortable hosting an event, you might want to have a session for practice conversations. Meet with several friends and ask them to help you role-play. Practice involving your "non-Christian" friend in conversation about his or her children, job, hobbies. You might bring up topics from last night's newspaper or ask about your guest's interests and concerns. Avoid discussing church or Christian subjects, which might alienate a non-Christian.

Although these practice conversations might seem awkward, they will prepare you for talking with people at the "real thing."

8. Gather Your Materials

What will you need to bring to your event? Order enough copies of the *Four Spiritual Laws* to give one to each person at the party. You can obtain them at your Christian bookstore or use the order information in the Resources section at the back of this book. You also will need name tags and a small table on which to put them, as well as 3×5 cards and pencils for comments and a basket to hold them. If you are planning a demonstration or lesson such as a craft activity, make a list of those materials as well.

If this is your first experience in life sharing, these eight steps may seem overwhelming. Once you have hosted a few gatherings in your home, however, the steps will become easier and more natural for you. We encourage you to adapt these suggestions to your event, then relax and enjoy the planning.

Creative Vision

Many times, we miss opportunities to reach out that are right under our noses. Once you feel comfortable hosting life-sharing events, ask God to show you other places as opportunities to minister.

Recently, I was visiting my mother, Mrs. Dan Lee. She lives in a lovely retirement home called Constitution House in Aurora, Illinois.

Mother and I were sharing how God works in our daily lives. We reminisced about how my grandfather and his brother each came to know Christ in their 20s. Right after their decisions, they covenanted together to pray for their children and grandchildren. As they grew older, they had the privilege of watching family members come into the kingdom of God. As a result of their example, Mother is always open to sharing her faith. For instance, she introduced a young wife to Christ. This young woman and her husband had been on drugs and their home was in disarray. Mom prayed and became actively involved in their lives. She taught the young woman to cook, clean, and manage her home. They prayed for her husband and he eventually received Christ also. Today they are active members in Mother's church.

As Mother and I visited, she said, "I haven't shared my faith with many of my neighbors in Constitution House." So we prayed and decided to host an Easter brunch. I delivered invitations to her neighbors. We cooked together and had such fun!

When the guests arrived, we served the food and spent time getting acquainted with each of them. Then I briefly shared a Christian poem and gave each person a plastic egg that held a Scripture verse. As our guests left, we knew we had made new friends and Mom was excited about reaching out further.

Recently, I visited Mom again. The women who had come to the brunch greeted me warmly, and each one wanted me to know what that special day meant to them. What will God lead Mom to do next? She is ready, waiting for God's direction!

I challenge you to find places to share your faith that you never considered before. Is there a retirement home near where you live? How about an apartment complex? Do you have a shut-in friend who would like to reach out to her neighbors—with your help? How about working mothers in your office? Do they need a night out—with babysitting provided? Ask God to give you a vision for places around you that others have forgotten.

If you have followed these suggestions, your planning is complete and you're ready to begin.

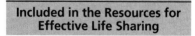

Included in the Resources for Effective Life Sharing

❧ Hostess Checklist

❧ Invitations and Menu Ideas

CHAPTER 8

The Time Has Arrived

Vonette

ALICE MCINTIRE also loves a party. I have learned so much from her. Every party she gives has a touch of the spectacular with elegance. Whether the event is in her home or someone else's and she has a part in the planning, it will likely be a remarkable event.

Alice looks for ways to attract the non-Christian that will impress them with the person of Christ and uses everything she has to God's honor and glory. Perhaps that is the reason God has blessed her with so much ability and material wealth.

For years, her husband was not a believer, but he encouraged her to be active in church, hold Bible classes in her home, and help finance Christian events. Although it was not easy living with a person who did not fully share her joy, she maintained her testimony, taught her son to love the Lord, and eventually they led Alice's husband to trust Christ.

Alice has taught Bible classes in the La Jolla, San Diego, and Rancho Santa Fe areas of southern California for more than fifty years. She also has had a part in almost every significant Christian event near her, from assisting with Billy Graham crusades in San Diego to planting new churches in that area. At ninety-one, she still teaches a Bible class with an assistant whom she trained. She is still one of the most attractive, vivacious women I know and is most concerned that people come into a personal relationship with Christ.

Alice's trademark is hats. She collects them, and she wears them well to luncheons and to church. All of her friends, of whom I am one, know where to borrow a hat for any special occasion.

A couple of years ago, Alice and her Bible class decided to host a "hat tea." Guests were asked to wear a special hat—funny, creative, or beautiful—and to bring a non-Christian woman. Alice had asked one of her guest's husbands to judge which hat was best in each category and prizes would be awarded to the winners.

Two days before the tea, as Alice was getting out of the back seat of a friend's car, she tripped in her patent-leather high-heeled shoes and fell. Her face hit the curb, resulting in several colorful bruises. But Alice didn't say a word to her prospective guests. The Lord's party was still on, and since she had performed for many years as a monologist in Hollywood, she knew an experienced make-up artist who made her bruises practically vanish.

Alice had decorated her home beautifully, and when we arrived in our hats for the tea, we felt we were sailing into a pink cloud. The food tables in the house and on the patio were fabulous, including pink divinity, which is Alice's favorite item at any party. Alice greeted us wearing a pink lace suit with matching hat and shoes.

Dr. Lloyd Ogilvie, now chaplain of the U.S. Senate, presented a great message that gave an opportunity for commitment to Christ. The society-page editor and photographer from the local newspaper covered the party, featuring a full page of pictures that identified Alice's party as one of the social events of the season. The article even mentioned a follow-up Bible study that was planned.

The response to the message was enthusiastic. During the entire event, Alice honored the Lord in all of her remarks and in her humor, and she made the tea a memorable event for everyone.

Perhaps you will never host an event that attracts the press or a government figure. But now that your guests will soon arrive, you can enjoy yourself as much as we did at Alice's "hat tea." The secret to having fun at your event is thorough planning and knowing how to conduct the party.

Before Your Guests Arrive

Let's think back and look at what needs to be done before the doorbell rings. As we mentioned earlier, complete as many tasks as you can beforehand. Arrange the room so that your speaker can be seen by everyone, so a window doesn't distract your audience or create glare, and so latecomers can join the group without disturbing others. You may also want to put on some soft background music to relax your guests. Review the introduction you prepared earlier for your speaker.

A lovely table can dress up any room. Select an artistic centerpiece. Of course, fresh flowers always fit the occasion, but consider other ideas as well, such as using a porcelain piece or a plant. If your table sits against a wall, position a one-sided arrangement toward the back of the table; if your table is free-standing, use a round or oblong two-sided centerpiece, depending on the table size and shape.

In the Resources, we have provided suggestions for centerpieces, invitations, and menus. You also can obtain many interesting and creative ideas for decorating from the dozens of magazines on the market. They are especially helpful with seasonal table-setting suggestions and special arrangements for door hangings, centerpieces, mantel decorations, and so forth. Have fun looking around and then adapt the ideas you like to fit your own circumstances.

If you expect a large crowd, serve from both sides of the food table. Set plates where they can be taken first, then place the food from the least to most important dish or dessert. Place your silverware, napkins, and drinks where they can be picked up last. This makes it easier for your guests to manage their plates and cups without spilling anything. Ask a hostess to sit at the end of the table to serve coffee and tea. You may also want to provide a separate punch table. If you have someone serving punch, that person should stand at the table rather than sit.

Now it is time to admire your table and look carefully at your arrangements to see if you have missed any last-minute details. Refer to your host checklist and ask your team to pray with you. Review with them your proposed schedule, which may look something like this:

> 20–30 minutes: Conversation and refreshments
> 30–45 minutes: Speaker's talk
> 20 minutes: More conversation

Remind your helpers to initiate conversation with people after the speaker concludes the message. Have them ask direct questions such as: "What did you think of the talk?" "Did it make sense to you?" "Have you made the wonderful discovery of knowing Christ personally? You would like to, wouldn't you?" Make sure that some of your helpers know how to lead a person to Christ.

To maintain your composure, sit quietly for the last ten minutes before your party. If you run around anxious and frazzled, you may set a negative tone. When the doorbell first rings, put hot coffee and tea on the table. Also take the telephone off the hook, or station someone nearby to answer it as soon as it rings. Then enjoy your guests.

Hosting the Event

When your guests arrive, greet them warmly at the door. Ask your speaker to stand with you so you can introduce him or her. Say something like: "(Speaker's name), this is (guest's name). Her children and mine are good friends." To the guest, "(Speaker's name) will be sharing with us today. (Guest's name), this is (speaker's name). She and I play tennis together every Tuesday afternoon."

If you have a large group, provide name tags already made out and placed on a nearby table for easy access. As soon as you finish greeting a guest, direct him or her to the name-tag table and to the table for food and drinks. You may, however, choose to make the name tags available before your guests enter the receiving line.

If your event is a dinner party, have hors d'oeuvres ready for your guests to enjoy as they arrive. One of your team members can direct your guests to the refreshments and other helpers can pour coffee and tea and replenish the table. If you have a small group, as hostess you may be able to manage these responsibilities alone.

If you are serving a sophisticated crowd, consult an etiquette book or an experienced hostess for the correct way to pour coffee and tea. Usually, the person who pours is seated at the end of the table with cups placed around the coffee service. Do not stack cups. As a guest approaches, put a coffee cup on the tray and pour the coffee. Place the cup of coffee on the guest's plate.

If you purchased the cake or dessert from a bakery, ask them how to slice it properly. If the cake has thick icing or is messy to handle, have someone serve it. Set a small plate and knife beside the cake to scrape the cutting knife when it becomes coated with icing. Cut one piece of cake at a time and set it out on a plate or place it on a guest's plate.

Encourage the host or hostess to involve non-Christians in conversation to which they can contribute. Focus on your guests instead of talking about yourself.

After twenty or thirty minutes, ask your guests to be seated and place the "Welcome, come on in" sign on the outside of the front door. Once guests are comfortable, formally introduce your speaker. In your introduction, mention things that she has in common with many of your guests since that will help the audience relate to her. Emphasize your speaker so that your listeners will focus on her. Say little about yourself.

After the talk, it is best to have the speaker present the gospel and the comment cards. He or she has built a bond with the audience and can easily transition into the *Four Spiritual Laws* booklet or other gospel presentation. Barbara and I recommend using the *Four Spiritual Laws* because it is a clear, simple presentation of the gospel. Also, you can provide booklets for each person to take home to read later.

If for some reason your speaker doesn't make the gospel clear, review it with your audience either by reading through the *Four Spiritual Laws* booklet with them or by reemphasizing the four points. A transition you could use is:

I'm sure you've enjoyed hearing about our speaker's introduction to the Christian life and how Jesus has changed her. Now I would like to give each of you a booklet that has been very helpful to millions of people, and to go over the contents with you. I'd like to do this for two reasons: First, although you may know what you believe, you may not know how to share your beliefs with others. Second, you may not know how to have a personal relationship with God but would like to understand.

Then read through the booklet with your guests. The Resources contain a section titled, "How to Present the *Four Spiritual Laws*," which gives detailed information on how to read through the booklet with a group. Also, Chapter 12 explains how to help guests receive Christ through prayer.

If for some reason your speaker does not ask the guests to fill out their comment cards, you can handle that. Some people like to hand out the *Four Spiritual Laws* booklets and comment cards at the beginning as guests are seated. However, we prefer to have the speaker or host distribute these right after the personal testimony so guests won't be distracted by them during the speaker's talk.

In closing the message part of your event, ask your guests to write their name and address on the card as well as any comments or questions they have about the talk. Also ask them to place an "X" beside their name if they just received Christ through prayer.

If you are planning a Bible study or other follow-up, mention the date it will be held, location, and time. Encourage your guests to attend the study to learn more about Jesus Christ and how He can change their lives. Then ask your guests to fold their cards in half and place them in a bowl or basket that you have set in a convenient place.

The comment card will serve two vital purposes: first, to reveal your guests' needs and reactions to the event; second, to disclose how many people prayed to receive Christ for the first time. This is not just for your own information, but to identify future ministry opportunities.

After giving guests time to fill out their cards, the speaker should thank the host or hostess, offer more refreshments, and initiate a conversation with someone nearby to eliminate an awkward silence.

As host, you can also invite the guests to help themselves to more coffee, tea, and dessert. Then you and your team members can make yourselves available to people who may have questions or needs.

After your guests leave, meet with your team to review the comment cards. Then begin planning how you will follow up your event. Chapter 9 will help you plan and implement this part of the life-sharing process.

Barbara and I have found that people really enjoy themselves at these events. We have received many heart-warming comments, both on the cards and in person. And when some of our guests receive Christ or decide to begin growing in their faith, our joy really does overflow.

But perhaps you're thinking, *That's great. You and Barbara are experienced hostesses. When I try to put on a simple event, something always goes wrong.* Well, let me tell you that both Barbara and I have had our share of interesting experiences, and these too can be used by God as you trust Him to enable you to handle them appropriately.

What to Do When Things Go Wrong

Let me share with you some of the events that almost turned into catastrophes.

One of the largest parties I held was for Henrietta Mears. Earlier, I had helped plan a bridal shower for Colleen Townsend, a young actress who married Louis Evans, Jr., who became pastor of the National Presbyterian Church in Washington, D.C. Miss Mears was so impressed with the refreshments I made that she asked if I would do a tea for her. Of course, I was delighted.

This was before Bill and I lived with Miss Mears and I was still teaching full time, so I prepared everything at our house on Friday night and Saturday morning. I made tea sandwiches twenty-four hours in advance and used a trick I learned to keep them fresh. I laid the sandwiches close together on cookie sheets, covered them with wax paper, then with a damp towel. The towel kept the bread moist without giving it a stale taste. I had things pretty much under control.

Saturday afternoon, I carried the food to Miss Mears' house just before the guests were to arrive. The table looked gorgeous and everything was in place. Mrs. Shearer, the housekeeper, was making the tea according to the instructions I had given her. Suddenly, she called me to the kitchen, exclaiming, "Vonette, taste this tea. It's really terrible. We can't serve it like this!"

It tasted very bitter. We checked my recipe, and Mrs. Shearer had followed it exactly. So I said, "Let's pray."

I asked the Lord, "You turned the water into wine at Cana. Now we ask You to do something with this tea. Amen."

Immediately, the idea came to mind to add sugar. We added just the right amount and got many compliments on how great the tea tasted. While replenishing the food table, Mrs. Shearer and I laughed in the kitchen about what God had done with that tea.

Another evening, we had a dinner party at Arrowhead Springs. After our guests arrived, smoke from the fireplace began filling the room. At first we couldn't determine what was happening, but then we discovered that a downdraft had caused the problem.

We couldn't go on with our party like this, and pouring water into the fireplace certainly wouldn't eliminate the smoke. So Bill and I asked the Lord for wisdom. We decided to take the burning log outside by rigging up a metal contraption lined with foil. With the help of about half of our guests, we carried the log out.

There was nothing to do but laugh at the situation. Even now, Bill and I occasionally run into someone who was at our home that evening and mentions that memorable party.

Bill and I have had perfectly clear California skies turn into quick showers on the day we planned an outside event. Once we had set tables, chairs, dinner service, and napkins for 150 to 200 guests when, without notice, we had a brief shower of rain. When our guests arrived, we explained what had happened, and everyone graciously took napkins and wiped off the chairs and plates.

We provided dry napkins, but made do with damp tablecloths. However, our spirits weren't dampened—we had a wonderful time.

Occasionally you must be flexible with your situation and make the best of it. Never panic or think that your party is ruined. Instead, quickly pray about your crisis, then make it into a memory. Some of the worst situations are the ones that God turns into the greatest ministry opportunities.

Well, we've come a long way in our journey toward life sharing. I am sure you still have doubts and questions. But the moment your guests arrive and you begin to minister to them, the Lord will use your willingness to serve others in ways you will not expect.

Alice McIntire and others like her who wish to introduce their friends to Christ through entertaining know from years of experience the joy of hospitality. You will, too, as God gives you creative ideas on how to use what He has given you to touch the lives of others.

Your life-sharing event will lead you into wonderful follow-up opportunities. In the next chapter, we'd like to help you begin a Bible study that will help you expand your ministry throughout your neighborhood, workplace, or community. We will show you how to build bridges to follow-up on your guests and to lead a small group. As you do so, your Bible study will also become an effective way to reach non-Christians with the good news.

Included in the Resources for Effective Life Sharing

❧ Invitations and Menu Ideas

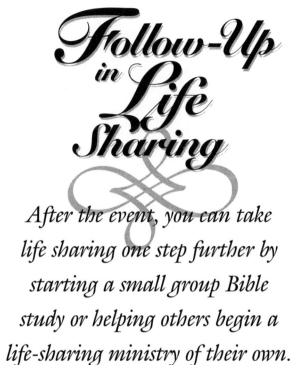

Follow-Up in Life Sharing

After the event, you can take life sharing one step further by starting a small group Bible study or helping others begin a life-sharing ministry of their own.

CHAPTER 9

Helping Others to Mature Spiritually

Barbara

NOW THAT YOU'VE had your life-sharing event, you are probably wondering what comes next. Life sharing is not a one-time happening; it opens doors for other ministry opportunities. The next step is to follow-up on people who receive Christ or Christians who are excited about living closer to God. You can do this through a small group Bible study.

Involving new Christians in Bible study, group prayer, and fellowship will almost guarantee their spiritual growth. Through a Bible study group, you can reach out to other neighbors and friends who haven't yet attended a life-sharing event. You multiply your efforts by training others to develop their own ministry. You can show them how simple it is to be a host, to prepare a personal testimony, and to speak at an event. I've seen tremendous things happen through Bible study groups. Let me share a testimony from Mary Jane Morgan of how exciting a Bible study can be.

Mary Jane Morgan

From an early age, I wanted to be a wife and rear a family. Although I married a wonderful man, Jim, and had three children, things didn't turn out exactly like I thought they would. My responsibilities were more difficult than I expected. I began to feel guilty about not having enough patience and felt anxious and empty inside.

Knowing deep down that God was the answer, I attended my church more often. But that didn't help.

About that time, someone invited me to a neighborhood Bible study. I went because it was in a home rather than a church. I would never have gone to a church different from the one in which I was reared.

The teacher's name was Marty Mandt. Through her teaching and example, I came to Christ. The Bible study grew and grew, and in time it ended up in my home.

Knowing Christ made all the difference in the world to me because that's when I realized that I was doing the will of God as a wife and mother. And Marty taught us how to live the Spirit-filled life right from the beginning. She showed me how to be the right kind of wife, mother, and neighbor.

I had a good friend named Ruth Bates. I tried and tried to get her to the Bible class, but she wouldn't come. Then one summer, Jim and I traveled to Europe. Ruth and Loring, her husband, were supposed to go with us, but financial reverses made them cancel their plans. While we were in Europe, Ruth's teenage son, Lo, went camping. He climbed a tree and fell, then waited six hours before coming home. When he arrived, he was very sick.

Ruth was frantic. Her husband was a Christian Scientist, so he did not take Lo to the hospital. The responsibility rested on Ruth.

The doctors discovered that Lo's spleen had burst and he was hemorrhaging internally. They operated immediately. Ruth waited by Lo's beside until the hospital staff insisted she go home and rest.

Later as she got into bed, her body started trembling so badly that the whole bed shook. She cried out, "Loring, what can I do?" Then she thought, *I'll pray.* She didn't know how to talk to God, but she knew the Lord's Prayer and repeated it aloud. A miraculous calm descended over her, and she fell asleep.

The next morning, Ruth rushed back to the hospital. She found out that Lo had begun hemorrhaging again during the night. The nurses were preparing him for a second operation when the bleeding mysteriously stopped. Ruth was astonished to find out that this happened at the very same time that she had prayed!

When Jim and I returned from our travels, we went to Ruth's house and heard all about Lo's surgery and Ruth's prayer. She looked at me and said, "Mary Jane, I want to go to that Bible class."

I was amazed. She had refused for two years, but now God had used this crisis to open her heart. Of course, Ruth received Christ through that study!

Later, Jim and I took another trip to Europe. Right after we returned, I received a call from our travel agent, Mary. "I'd like you to meet with a lady who's thinking about making a trip to Europe. Her name is Nina Locke. Would you have lunch with us?"

"Yes, I will."

I thought, *Perhaps God wants me to give my testimony to Nina.* So I came to the restaurant with my *Four Spiritual Laws.*

Nina was gorgeous and dressed like a model. We introduced ourselves and started talking. When Mary called the restaurant to say she would be late, Nina and I kept chatting. I never asked her about her spiritual life because I thought she had everything together in her life. When Mary arrived, we all went in to lunch.

Five minutes after we sat down, Mary mentioned the Bible class I attended. Nina looked up and said, "A Bible class?"

I told her when and where it was held. She brought out a little notebook and wrote down the information. Not only did she show up at the next Bible study, she received Christ that day.

I found out later that the day before we met, Nina had thrown herself on her bed and cried, "God, I need help! You show me the way." But having never attended a church or grown up in a home where the Bible was read, she had no idea what to do. Yet God graciously answered her prayer through that Bible study.

Nina was so hungry for God that she read everything anyone gave her. Her life changed so much that her family noticed. Her children began saying, "The day our mother went to Bible study, she came back a different person."

In time, Ruth, Nina, and I took turns teaching that small Bible class and began hosting evangelistic coffees in our homes. We all worked and prayed together. Marty taught us how to win our husbands to Christ the biblical way. Couples' classes were started and Nina's husband received Christ six months after Nina did. Jim, my husband, also asked Christ to come into his life.

Ruth's husband, Loring, had a more difficult time because of his Christian Science beliefs. But they had a happy marriage because she obeyed God in her relationship with her husband. Then three years ago, Loring received Christ on his deathbed. That was an answer to prayer for all of us! And all this happened because Marty was faithful to teach a small Bible class in a home.

Barbara

Mary Jane's experience isn't an isolated case. I've seen Bible studies produce these kinds of results over and over again. A new Christian begins to grow in faith because a friend takes a personal, loving interest. In fact, holding small group training is not something new, it was how Jesus taught His disciples.

Following the Example of Jesus

Jesus is our example in all of life. As we come to Him in our daily living, He teaches us and leads us in His ways. He comes alongside and helps us walk in His footsteps. A dear friend gave me a poem that explains this growth process and how faithful God is to continue the work He has begun in each of us.

The Road of Life

At first, I saw God as my observer, my judge,
keeping track of the things I did wrong,
so as to know whether I merited heaven
or hell when I die.
He was out there sort of like a president.
I recognized His picture when I saw it,
but I really didn't know Him.

But later on
when I met Christ,
it seemed as though life were rather like a bike ride,
but it was a tandem bike,
and I noticed that Christ
was in the back helping me pedal.

I don't know just when it was
that He suggested we change places,
but life has not been the same since.

When I had control,
I knew the way.
It was rather boring,
but predictable...
It was the shortest distance between two points.

I worried and was anxious and asked,
"Where are you taking me?"
He laughed and didn't answer,
and I started to learn to trust.

I forgot my boring life
and entered into the adventure.
And when I'd say, "I'm scared,"
He'd lean back and touch my hand.
He took me to people with gifts that I needed,
gifts of healing,
acceptance,
and joy.
They gave me gifts to take on my journey,
my Lord's and mine.

And we were off again.
He said, "Give the gifts away;
they're extra baggage, too much weight."
So I did
to the people we met,
and I found that in giving I received,
and still our burden was light.

I did not trust Him
at first,

in control of my life,
I thought He'd wreck it;

but He knows bike secrets,
knows how to make it bend to take sharp corners,
knows how to jump to clear high rocks,
knows how to fly to shorten scary passages.

And I am learning to shut up and pedal
in the strangest, darkest, loneliest places,
and I'm beginning to enjoy the view
and the cool breeze on my face
with my delightful constant companion, Jesus Christ.

And when I'm sure I just can't do anymore,
He just smiles and says... "Pedal."

—Author Unknown

Jesus came alongside and helped His disciples grow up in Him. If you trace His ministry through the first four books of the New Testament, you will see how He taught His friends, spent time with them, and helped them grasp eternal principles through His example. When they failed, He picked them up and encouraged them. When they disobeyed God's commands, He corrected them.

In my growth as a new Christian, I faltered in simply following Jesus. I quickly learned how to please other Christians by doing external "good works." For example, I went through my party clothes and gave many of them away. I destroyed my jazz records because I thought that would look good.

One day, while Howard and I were sitting in church, I noticed my long, red fingernails. *I shouldn't have these,* I thought and curled my fingers into a fist.

Howard whispered, "What are you doing?"

"As a Christian, I don't think I should have these long, red nails."

He wisely whispered back, "If you're hiding your nails from people, you're succeeding. But if you're hiding them from God, guess what?"

I realized that having long nails did not make me less godly. Howard and I laughed later and have chuckled over this many times since. I have related this incident to encourage new Christians to follow Jesus in their innermost attitudes—and Him alone!

When I was caught up in doing external good works, one of my dearest friends, Jane Newquist, said during that time, "Barbara, I liked you better before you became whatever you are now!" What a negative witness I was to her!

I finally realized that my attitude of doing the right thing to please people caused me to act in my own strength, but God wanted me to depend upon His strength so that He could lead me into His plan for me.

One of my heroes in the Old Testament is Eliezer, Abraham's servant. He was sent to find a bride for Abraham's son, Isaac. When Eliezer prayed for the right woman to be at the well, his prayer was miraculously answered. He was so excited that before he sat down to dinner with the woman's family, he shared about his God. He bowed his head and worshipped the Lord and said, "Blessed be the Lord…I being in the way [of obedience and faith] the Lord led me to the house of my master's kinsmen" (Genesis 24:27, Amplified). How simple; how true. Pleasing people is a weakness of mine. I would rather be in the way of obedience and faith so God can lead me!

That's why I am so grateful that Vonette took the time to help me mature in my faith. I call this ministry Coming Alongside. Just as Jesus did with His disciples, we can walk hand-in-hand with those we introduce to Christ, showing them how to study their Bibles, how to pray, and how to apply biblical principles in their lives. As you encourage others and work with them, you will find many reasons for Coming Alongside in life sharing.

Why Follow-Up Is So Important

The next time you admire a piece of pottery, think of the craftsmanship and time that went into its lines and colors. The potter transforms a formless blob of clay into a piece of art. He begins by gently squeezing the air bubbles out of the clay so that the pottery won't explode in the kiln. The clay is centered on a pottery wheel, which gives the clay a sturdy base. As the wheel turns, the potter expertly shapes the clay into the piece he has in mind. Finally, the piece is left to dry before being glazed in brilliant colors.

This depicts what happens when we trust our life to Christ. Isaiah writes, "O Lord, you are our Father. We are the clay and you are the Potter. We are all formed by your hand" (Isaiah 64:8, TLB). The moment we yield ourselves to the heavenly Potter, the Holy Spirit begins shaping us into the image of Christ.

We can have a part in this process in others. Although God is the Master Potter, He has given us the privilege of helping to shape lives through His power.

But often, we leave new Christians to find their way alone. We assume they automatically will go to church, study their Bible, tell others of their newfound faith, and pray daily. Sometimes one will, but that is rare. Although these new believers love the Lord, usually they become discouraged and don't mature into fruitful Christians.

Follow-up enables new Christians to learn from the example of other believers, through getting to know them and watching how they practice their faith. Young believers begin to build relationships with people who will encourage them where they are weak and will help them solve their problems God's way.

Spiritual maturity must be developed over time; it cannot be put on like a garment. New Christians need direction to know what God's Word says and how to apply its principles to their particular situations. And, of course, they need to learn how to share their faith. In a Bible study, members can see how others introduce friends, neighbors, and loved ones to Jesus, and they will begin to understand how to pray for people for whom they have a concern.

Encouraging others to reach out is a natural part of life-sharing Bible studies. Recently, I was involved in a group that illustrates this principle. I hosted a six-week, small-group Bible study in my home. The women who had attended were interested in getting together for further study. I knew of a Bible study led by Sally Clingman so I suggested that we all go together.

Later, I asked three of these women to help with an Easter brunch. They were enthusiastic as we planned our brunch. We invited Sally to speak and sent out the invitations. The brunch was great! People felt comfortable and when Sally spoke, I could see openness and even tears on many faces.

One of the women received Christ and many more responded positively to the event. Several began attending Sally's Bible study and others came to a study at my home.

I take joy in the promise God gives in Philippians 1:6 that the work He has begun in our lives He will continue until the day Jesus returns to earth. So the process continues—God faithfully brings people to Himself, and those who have received Christ in life-sharing events reach out to others by having parties and gatherings of their own. That's spiritual multiplication in action!

Building Relationships

As we learned earlier, making friends and building relationships begins before a life-sharing event. You can learn about your guests' lives as you invite them, and engage new people in conversation while you host the party. But the real relationship building occurs after the event is over. Not only does a Bible study enable you to build a relationship with new Christians and others in your group, but it also encourages other members to get to know each other.

New Christians are usually eager to make friends with believers. The Christian life is new to them, and they have a fresh love for their Lord. But their old lives may include habits or circumstances that will tempt them back into old sinful patterns.

When you talk to new believers or to worldly Christians who want to change their ways, listen carefully. Perhaps you have never experienced some of the problems your friend has, but a listening ear can go a long way toward healing the hurts.

Remind your new brother or sister in the Lord to read the Bible and pray daily and to attend church. Show him or her how you have a quiet time. Then pray and read the Bible together. Many new Christians face temptations they never encountered before. Teach them how to resist the enemy and follow Christ sincerely.

When your friend encounters problems, assure him or her that God is sovereign and that He is the one who encourages us and helps us handle our difficulties. He produces our spiritual growth (1 Corinthians 3:5,6).

Be careful that you don't consider this person your "assignment." Instead, build a sincere friendship. Take your friend to a ball game or go shopping at the mall. New Christians need to talk about what God is teaching them in an environment of acceptance.

Love your new friends unconditionally. That's the best way to demonstrate God's love for them. Forgive them for their failings, encourage them, and refrain from criticizing. Of course, there is a place for Scriptural correction, but do this in an attitude of love and tenderness. Ask the Holy Spirit to empower and control your life as you relate with them.

How to Begin Your Follow-Up

Comment cards are the key to beginning follow-up. As soon as your guests leave your life-sharing event, meet with your helpers and review the cards. Note the names of those who expressed interest in a Bible study or who have placed an "X" on the card to indicate that they received Christ. Pray for these people right away.

The next day, send a letter to each new believer or get together with him or her. A sample letter is provided in the Resources. Be sincere in your offer to help them in whatever way you can.

Some people who indicate interest on their comment cards will not follow through with a commitment. Even the Lord experienced this during His ministry on earth. But you will find new believers who really desire to grow in their faith and who want to learn how to study the Bible and pray.

Within two weeks of your event, call to arrange a meeting with those who have further questions or who indicated they had received Christ. In the Resources, Vonette and I have included a helpful chart on how to conduct that first telephone call. The chart gives tips on how to establish rapport, bring up a discussion of spiritual subjects, and close the conversation. Study the chart until you are familiar with the process, then make your first call. Soon you'll be an expert at beginning your follow-up.

After the call, you may want to send a short note confirming your appointment, especially if it is a week or more away or if the person seemed uncertain about meeting with you. If the person you contacted had a time conflict but didn't seem antagonistic to getting together, send a note expressing your disappointment and hope that you can meet in the future. You may want to include your written testimony and perhaps another booklet. Record the date of your conversation and invite that person to another event in a week or two. Keep in touch as long as you receive a positive response. Try to prevent closing the door to a relationship.

Before you meet with the person who came to your life-sharing event, ask the Holy Spirit to fill you with His power and wisdom. Then relax. You aren't just imparting facts, you are introducing someone to the greatest person who ever lived—Jesus Christ. It's not your responsibility to "make" your new friend receive Christ as Savior or grow in his or her faith. Simply take the initiative to share the gospel in the power of the Holy Spirit, then leave the results to God (1 Thessalonians 1:5).

As you go for your appointment, take two copies of the *Four Spiritual Laws* booklet so both of you can read it at the same time. Because they don't understand what God has promised in His Word, many new Christians—and even more mature believers—lack assurance that Christ is in their life. During the appointment, review the information in the booklet and spend most of your time on the portion that helps assure believers that Christ is in their life. The questions in the booklets are: Did you ask Christ into your life? Where is Christ right now?

As you talk together and enjoy yourselves, don't forget that people are busy and you should limit the time of your meeting to an hour.

After you have concluded your presentation of the gospel, ask your friend to attend church with you and invite him or her to your upcoming Bible study. Since people learn more from seeing your life than from hearing your words, spend time with your friend. For those who haven't yet responded to Christ's love, look for additional ways to show loving interest in them and continue building the bridge of personal relationship.

Leading a Bible Study

Soon it will be time for your Bible study. Several people have said they want to attend. You have set the time and place. Now, I'd like to challenge you to consider leading the study. I have seen many Christians who thought they could never manage this role, but who do very well when they lead a Bible study. They found tremendous blessing in building spiritual values into others' lives and training them to reach out with life-sharing events.

When I had been a Christian for just one year, some women in the community asked me to lead a Bible study. I knew very little Scripture, but they urged me, so I finally said yes.

Ann, one of the women who attended, was a wonderful watercolor artist. Since she also knew a lot about the Bible, she often corrected me in what I had presented. At those times, I wished she would teach the study. I wanted to quit.

One day, I brought a message on a card that explained how to be filled with the Holy Spirit. It gave the simple steps on how to breathe spiritually.

1. Confess: 1 John 1:9
2. Receive: Ephesians 5:18
3. Believe: 1 John 5:14,15

I suggested that the women do what I did—tape the card up on my kitchen window and ask God daily for the infilling of the Holy Spirit in my life.

A couple nights later, Ann called me. She was crying and talking excitedly. She told me that although she knew a lot of biblical facts, she lacked the Holy Spirit's reality in her life. When she read the card, she had said, "Of course! That's so simple!" and asked to be filled with the Spirit. That changed her life. Later, she shared her experience with the other women in the group.

When Howard and I moved from Illinois to California, Ann gave me two of her paintings. We have treasured those paintings, hanging them in a place of honor in each home we have owned.

In that Bible study I learned a principle that has been part of my ministry ever since. First Thessalonians 5:24 says, "The one who calls you is faithful and he will do it." Once again, God showed me that He is not limited to my capabilities. I would have missed a blessing if I had given up during that first Bible study.

I encourage you to be open to this leadership position. Ask God to show you whether leading a Bible study is a ministry He would like you to adopt. Then observe a Bible study to see how the leader guides the students through the lesson. In the Resources, we have included a section on "How to Lead a Small Group Bible Study," and have listed effective Bible study materials.

When you lead your first study, don't be overly concerned with the number in the group. Jesus said, "Where two or three come together in my name, there am I with them" (Matthew 18:20). Whether one student comes or a dozen, a faithful teacher will realize that God enables him to encourage others to grow in their faith and to begin reaching out to unbelievers with His love.

Create a friendly environment in your group. Holding the study in a home helps set the tone. A genuine spirit of love and acceptance will allow your study to be a haven from daily stress and strain. Be sensitive about how God is working in group members' lives, and follow-up on prayer requests. During the meeting, ask individuals to pray for the needs expressed. Report answers to prayer, and praise God for what He is doing.

As you come alongside, you will discover that, although you teach a group of students the same material, each individual is unique and will have different questions. In your follow-up, remember that the person is more important than the program.

Plan life-sharing events to encourage your members to begin reaching their friends and neighbors. Be sure to schedule times for fun where you can help build fellowship within your group.

Have we given you a taste for how exciting a Bible study can be? One Sunday, Howard and I were in a couples' class led by Johnny and Anna Cash, friends of ours who live in Orlando. We began talking about how hospitable Mary and Martha in the Bible were and how Jesus enjoyed relaxing in their home.

The conversation naturally turned to how we use our homes for hospitality. Howard said, "Johnny, you give so much hospitality in your life."

Johnny looked surprised. Howard told him how he had observed Johnny meeting strangers with joy and warmth. "You listen and encourage, and your desire is to do God's will."

Anna replied, "He brings the people, and I entertain."

The other day, Howard and I received a written invitation to their third annual Golf Party for the neighborhood men. The invitation was followed by a call from Johnny.

The Sunday afternoon of the party, the sportsmen were rained out. But that didn't dampen Johnny and Anna's spirits for the dinner in the evening. When we arrived, chicken and hamburgers were on the grill. Name tags were given out and people were introduced. Everyone began to relax, and soon they were laughing and enjoying each other.

Before we sat around the table, Johnny called us into the family room and said, "Let's get into a circle, hold hands, and pray."

Later, we listened and laughed and deep conversations took place. Evangelism and fun are partners in building relationships. The love of Johnny and Anna and their caring enthusiasm for their neighbors made the difference. They are heroes of the faith to me!

Each of us can play a part in life sharing—from hosting events to leading Bible studies—whether we're married or single, male or female. Where do you fit in? Have you allowed God to perform His best in your life? I encourage you to seek God's will for reaching your neighborhood. Come alongside and find the joy of serving others in a way that will bring eternal changes.

**Included in the Resources for
Effective Life Sharing**

- ❧ Sample Follow-Up Letter
- ❧ Setting Up and Conducting a
  Follow-Up Appointment

CHAPTER 10

Demonstrating a Life-Sharing Event

Barbara

HOW DO YOU interest people in life sharing if they are afraid to invite others or to host an evangelistic gathering? How do you get someone excited about hosting a coffee, brunch, party, or dinner for their non-Christian friends? By demonstrating a life-sharing event in which they can see how easy and exciting it is to host an event.

Let me show you how your enthusiasm about using your home as a place for ministry can spread. I had shared with one of my Christian friends many times about how much fun life sharing can be. But she resisted, saying, "I feel awkward about doing something like this."

Then she attended a life-sharing demonstration coffee. She *saw* how enjoyable it was to greet people at the door, offer them refreshments, and talk to them. She *heard* the clear, nonthreatening way the gospel was presented by a woman who simply loved the Lord. As a result, my friend became excited about life sharing.

Recently, I attended an information outreach at a home in Statesville, North Carolina. Howard and I were helping to direct

113

a Lay Institute for Evangelism (LIFE), which is Campus Crusade's practical training in how to share the good news of Jesus Christ with others. As part of the seminar, held in a local church, the women were invited to attend a life-sharing demonstration. After the coffee was over, they were all enthusiastic. Here are some of their responses:

"Thanks for sharing in a relaxed, informal way."

"What a meaningful and wonderful morning you shared with us. Thanks for helping each of us to grow as Christians and to grow in loving relationships."

"I enjoyed seeing this done in such a simple way. Great!"

The concept of demonstrating a life-sharing event was developed over the years as LIFE seminars were held in churches across the United States. After the seminar, the staff members encouraged people to invite neighbors into their home, reach out with kindly acts, and build bridges to evangelism. (To receive more information about LIFE conferences, see the order information at the end of this book.) Evangelistic entertaining was the method for achieving these goals. We discovered that some Christians were reluctant to host a life-sharing coffee, brunch, or party after just hearing about it. But seeing a demonstration assured them that they could do it, too.

What is it about the training in a demonstration event that makes it so vital?

First, *seeing a women's coffee or a couples' party builds confidence* in those who desire to reach out into their neighborhood. You may have many Christians in your congregation or in your ministry group who hesitate to participate in life sharing because they are afraid to witness. Training helps them overcome their fears by teaching them the essentials of hosting the event and leading a person to Christ.

Second, *attending a coffee, brunch, or party demonstration gives prospective hosts and hostesses practical experience.* They discover how to greet guests, what kind of refreshments to serve, how to introduce a speaker, and how to begin follow-up. In experiencing each part of the event, some of the mystery and strangeness is lifted.

These ministering Christians can begin to see themselves as a host or greeter or perhaps a speaker.

Third, *the prospective host or hostess improves the effectiveness of his or her life-sharing skills.* Christians who attend discover new ways of extending hospitality. They learn how to give a more precise and clear presentation of God's good news. They observe how to talk to non-Christians about the Lord. And when they host their own event, they are not as easily thrown off track by a guest's questions.

During a life-sharing demonstration event, simply host the coffee or brunch as you would if you were inviting non-Christian guests. Hold the party in a home, or set up a room in your church to resemble a living room. Don't worry about the size of your group; just as in an actual life-sharing event, one or two people can be as effective as forty or fifty. The important consideration is that you ask God to bring the people He wants to attend your presentation. You could invite the leadership in your church, couples who want to reach out to non-Christians, or a particular ministry group, such as your church's women's ministry, Bible study members, or visitation committee.

This is a sample invitation you can adapt for your situation:

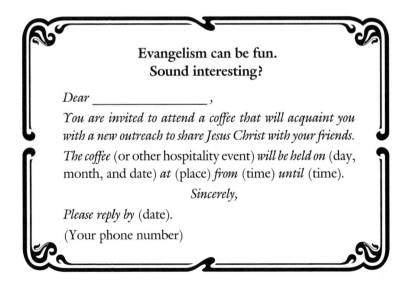

Evangelism can be fun.
Sound interesting?

Dear _____,

You are invited to attend a coffee that will acquaint you with a new outreach to share Jesus Christ with your friends.

The coffee (or other hospitality event) *will be held on* (day, month, and date) *at* (place) *from* (time) *until* (time).

Sincerely,

Please reply by (date).

(Your phone number)

Greet your guests as they arrive, just as you would for a "real" event. As you allow time for conversation, offer them refreshments and introduce them to the speaker. If you expect a large group, use the facilities in your church. Begin the coffee by saying, "Just imagine that I have invited you into my living room."

Then complete the remaining steps of your event, just as in a real party. The basic format is outlined in Chapters 6 through 8. The major parts include: formally introduce your speaker; have the speaker give his or her talk and present the gospel; provide an opportunity for non-Christians to receive Christ; and ask guests to fill out the comment cards.

Here is a sample participation card you might want to adapt for your life-sharing demonstration event and your situation:

Name _____

Address _____

City, Zip _____

Phone _____

Church _____

Comments:

☐ I would be interested in hosting an event.

☐ I will share this outreach with the people in my church.

Encourage each of your "guests" to fill out their comment cards as if they were participating in an actual event. After they finish writing, ask them to fold the cards in half and put them into a basket you have provided.

Then offer more refreshments. You might say, "Didn't you enjoy the speaker's presentation? The reason I have invited you here is to show you how easy and enjoyable it is to reach out to your neighbors through an event like this. Why don't we get some more coffee and cookies, then return to our seats in about ten minutes to discuss what you've just seen."

Give your guests ten minutes to get their refreshments and return to their seats. Then describe the basic format and purpose for a life-sharing party. Refer to Chapters 5 and 6 for information on reaching out to others. Encourage your guests to be involved in a life-sharing ministry, and invite them to ask questions. To help field these queries, let me share some of the most common questions I have been asked at demonstration events:

❧ **I don't see myself speaking. Can I be involved anyway?**

Yes. The opportunities for involvement are many. You could open your home for a coffee, tea, or dessert, or serve as a co-hostess in a friend's home. You could help make decorations or provide food. Volunteer to help wherever you feel most comfortable. As you participate in an event, you will become more confident about hosting your own.

❧ **Is this outreach always evangelistic?**

Yes. The whole purpose of entertaining evangelistically is to present the gospel in a clear way so that your non-Christian friends can respond to God's love. This book gives many variations on the kinds of events you can host, from children's and youth parties to Christmas gatherings and community functions.

❧ **I don't know many people outside my church. If I had a coffee, who would I invite?**

Do you live in a neighborhood? Then you have a ministry right at your doorstep. First, ask God to show you how to minister to your neighbors. Then take the initiative to meet them. Make a concerted effort to open your home and your life to them. You could invite them in for casual coffee or tea. Or plan a block party. The opportunities are unlimited.

❧ **Would entertaining evangelistically fit in with the women's ministry in my church?**

Yes! One of the simplest and easiest ways to share Christ is through your home. And many women have special gifts in hospitality. Inviting each woman to minister through her home encourages her to use her special gifts and abilities in her own way. Also, an evangelistic ministry like this doesn't take a great deal of finances or committees.

❧ Is this ministry limited to women?

No! The simple format for evangelistic entertaining fits all ages and groups. This ongoing type of ministry can include men, children, teens, seniors, couples, and singles. Anyone who has a home, condominium hospitality room, apartment community room, college facilities, or retirement home can invite neighbors in to hear the gospel presented.

❧ I'm excited about what God can do through a Christian's home. How can I get my friends excited about evangelistic entertaining?

You could begin by demonstrating an event in your home so that your friends can see how easy it is to open your home to others. Then invite them to help you host a gathering. Once your friends understand how simple it is, they can branch out by hosting their own coffees, teas, desserts, and parties.

❧ I have four children, and many times my house is disorderly. How can I ever clean it well enough to have my neighbors and friends in?

People do not come to a home because it is in perfect order. They want to be with warm, friendly people, and they will probably be more comfortable if it doesn't look like a show place. Instead of feeling apologetic about your home, concentrate on making people feel comfortable. Perhaps you could begin by being a co-hostess until you feel encouraged enough to host your own event.

❧ I like the format for life sharing, but frankly, it seems too simple. Wouldn't a more detailed program work better?

Life sharing is designed to be simple. If evangelistic entertaining were too well defined, we would not trust in God, but in our own plans. And a set format may not fit some events or neighborhood lifestyles.

❧ **I have needs myself. Sometimes I get angry and ornery around my house. How could I ever share my faith or minister to others?**

We are all sinners whom God graciously reconciled to Himself through the death of His Son. We can live our lives in front of people, letting them see our weaknesses, and therefore our spiritual growth. At the same time, many of our needs are met by reaching out to others.

Dr. Bill Bright says, "Joy comes from sharing your faith." When the demonstration party has ended, encourage guests to host their own coffee or brunch in the near future. Also, invite those who are already on a church leadership team or who direct the women's or evangelism committee in your church to plan a party. You might suggest an upcoming holiday, such as Christmas, Valentine's Day, Easter, Independence Day, or Thanksgiving, to host an initial life-sharing coffee or dessert. Brainstorm ways they could influence their neighborhoods, workplaces, and community.

Also, as you read the comment cards, note the names of those who wrote encouraging remarks. They are good candidates for hosting life-sharing events. Plan to contact them personally within a few days. Occasionally, you will find that a non-Christian has attended your demonstration event and has marked an "X" indicating that she has received Christ through prayer. Contact that person to make sure she understands what has happened and give her opportunities to grow in her faith.

Once someone in your group hosts a successful gathering, the enthusiasm for developing a home ministry will spread to others. If a Bible study is started, that can lead to even more desserts, teas, or couples' parties.

I encourage you to expand this vital ministry in your church or among your Christian friends. As you join with others to learn how to do evangelistic entertaining, you will develop an ever-increasing life-sharing ministry in your area!

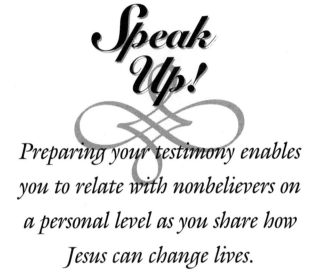

Speak Up!

Preparing your testimony enables you to relate with nonbelievers on a personal level as you share how Jesus can change lives.

CHAPTER 11

Preparing Your Personal Testimony

Barbara

A S A NEW Christian, giving my personal testimony seemed very strange to me. I enjoyed hearing how God had worked in other lives, but I felt threatened when it came to telling my own story because opening myself to others seemed too personal.

I was afraid to stand in front of others even in my grade school years. In high school, my public speaking teacher called me aside. "Barbara, now that the semester is over, I recommend that you forget you ever took this course. Don't pursue public speaking."

What a blow! But she was right. When asked to read aloud in class, I would nervously laugh in all the wrong places. Then I'd lose my concentration and my place in the reading. My words would get jumbled, and I'd feel thoroughly embarrassed.

One time the teacher sent me to the window because of my uncontrolled giggling. "Just stand there," she huffed, "and look outside until you can compose yourself enough to complete your speech."

With experiences like these engraved in my memory, I decided never to get into a speaking situation again.

After becoming a wife and mother, I involved myself in several social clubs and causes, but staunchly refused any position that required "up-front" responsibilities. I insisted that my talents were best used behind the scenes.

My fears didn't magically disappear when I became a Christian. In fact, I limited God's power in my life to my own capabilities. If I couldn't do something, then I didn't believe He could do it through me.

Several times my pastor asked me to give my testimony during one of the church services. "Oh, no," I protested, "my husband can do a much better job. I'm just no good at that sort of thing."

Perhaps you feel this way, too. For someone who does not feel comfortable in front of people, giving a personal testimony can be a catastrophic experience. But God meets all of our needs. Gaining confidence to share my faith started the day two friends from the Navigators ministry came by and shared with me how the apostle Paul gave his testimony in many different settings. They showed me how he used the same basic plan, but changed it to fit his audience.

In Acts 22, for example, Paul defended his life before his listeners. First he described his life *before* he received Christ as his Savior. As a devout Jew, he had persecuted Christians—even to the point of death. Then he told *how* he came to know Jesus on the road to Damascus, and how his life had changed *after* that experience. He became God's messenger to the unbelievers and a teacher to the new churches.

My friends then turned to Acts 26 and showed me how Paul had used the same formula to give his testimony a second time. As Paul stood before a Roman official named Agrippa, he once again went through a "before/how/after" outline.

My friends then encouraged me to write my testimony using the same simple plan. But I resisted.

Although I could not speak out, I had a heart for evangelism. Shortly after those caring women visited me, I decided to host a Christmas tea for my neighbors. I had no plan and no training in sharing my faith. But I called a neighbor, Jean Parent, and asked if she would help me with the food. She agreed. Dorothy Mahr, a friend from church who had a gorgeous voice, consented to sing at the tea.

We did it up fancy—brought out the silver and prepared holiday food. We sent out invitations—even to my Jewish neighbors. I nervously thought, *I hope all the women like this.*

And they did! In between her songs, Dorothy inserted appropriate Scriptures and told the Christmas story. I was brave enough to read "The Incomparable Christ," a writing on His life. Then I actually gave a brief testimony! I told the women that in the past year, God had become real to me. I was ecstatic at their response. And when I met my neighbors later, they commented on how special the Christmas tea was to them.

Paul told the Christians at Corinth, "When I came to you, brethren, I did not come with superiority of speech or of wisdom, proclaiming to you the testimony of God,...I was with you in weakness and in fear and in much trembling. And my message and my preaching were not in persuasive words of wisdom, but in demonstration of the Spirit and of power, that your faith should not rest on the wisdom of men, but on the power of God" (1 Corinthians 2:1–5, NASB).

God uses weak people to perform His work, and He enables the unlearned to spread His wisdom to unbelievers. Whatever your weakness, God wants to use you so that the world can see that God's power triumphs, not human strength!

Paul had described me perfectly. I too felt weak and fearful before my first scheduled speaking engagement. I had little confidence and a poor past record. My only hope was to trust God. He not only enabled me to give my testimony, but since then He has used my story many times to help bring others into His household.

But I still didn't know how to present the gospel clearly to others, so when I heard about Campus Crusade's planned training sessions in Wheaton, Illinois, I attended eagerly. I enjoyed the sessions on the ministry of the Holy Spirit and on how to introduce others to Jesus. A year later, Howard and I joined the staff of Campus Crusade. Part of new staff training is to write out a testimony. My trainer, Diane Ross Hutchinson, suggested an outline I could follow. It was the same before/how/after format that the apostle Paul used!

Now I do a lot of speaking at evangelistic events. God changed my life as I allowed Him to, and I know He can do the same for you. Even if you never plan to speak at an evangelistic coffee, I encourage you to put your testimony into words and become familiar with a simple gospel presentation. Then ask God to lead you to people with whom you can share your testimony.

A lack of confidence may reappear, as it has for me. This happened as I was sharing my testimony with a neighbor. I worried, *I must not be doing a very good job; she's not interested.* But I kept on. She didn't receive Christ that afternoon, but we continued our talks. Not everyone is ready the first time they hear about Christ's love, but your testimony will prepare their hearts for another time when they may be receptive.

If God can give me the power to overcome my shyness, then He can help you deal with whatever keeps you from being up front with your testimony. Vonette and I would like to help by showing you how to write your personal testimony, then give you tips on how to present it.

Why Write Out a Testimony?

You may be wondering, *Why should I write my personal testimony? Can't I just give it verbally?* There are several advantages to putting it on paper.

First, *it helps you see what God is doing in your life.* Without going through the process of thinking, writing, and revising, you may miss some of the gems God has produced in your life.

Second, *you will become so familiar with your testimony that you won't need notes or other aids to help you share it.* That will give you confidence and allow you to concentrate on the unbeliever or the group rather than on yourself.

Third, *seeing your testimony on paper will help you critique what you say.* You can judge better if it's too short or too long, or if it doesn't have enough substance.

Fourth, *you can give the same testimony time after time.* The before/how/after of your personal experience never changes. Your most recent spiritual growth is changing all the time and can be adapted to your audience. Determining the content of your testimony will help you avoid such problems as not giving enough information about how to receive Christ, using technical rather than simple language, and getting off the subject.

Fifth, from your written testimony, *you can work on your oral presentation to improve your speaking abilities.* We encourage Christians to practice in front of a mirror or videotape themselves giving their testimony to see how they look and sound to others.

Sixth, *you can ask others to evaluate your testimony.* They will help you sharpen your delivery and ensure that what you say comes through clearly. We have included an evaluation form in the Resources section that you can use for an evaluation time.

People cannot argue or disagree with someone's personal experience. That's why God can use your unique story to touch lives. Once it is written, you will be able to use your testimony with individuals you meet every day or with a group situation such as a life-sharing event.

Simplicity Works Best

Some time ago, the wife of a pediatrician invited Howard and me to speak at a couples' gathering in their home. Periodically, thirty-five or forty of their friends would get together to discuss various ideas. The woman thought Howard would be a good person to share the gospel with this group since he is so philosophical.

At the gathering, Howard introduced his talk by making this statement, "I have found that the best way to communicate to intelligent people is to make things as simple as possible." Then he went on to share his personal testimony. He explained how he had cried out to the Lord, "If you're in the life-changing business, here I am. Have at it."

After he finished telling how the Lord had changed his life, Howard then read through the *Four Spiritual Laws* booklet. When he concluded, we all had refreshments and enjoyed visiting. At one point, four couples gathered around us. We all joined hands and prayed as they invited Christ to control their lives.

Several years later, Howard and I were in the same area for a conference. The doctor who had hosted the earlier event approached us after the meeting. "Will you have lunch with me?" he insisted. "I have something to tell you."

The next day, we met him and his wife at a local restaurant. After we ordered our food, he announced, "You didn't know that the night you were in my home I invited Christ into my life, did you? I didn't even tell my wife right away. I decided not to change one thing in my life myself."

He continued by explaining that he had identified with Howard's simple cry to the Lord as a non-Christian. "I prayed the same thing!" the doctor exclaimed. "I figured that after I began to experience a few changes in my life, I would start to tell others about what happened to me."

For three months, he had kept silent. Finally, his wife asked, "What has happened to you? You're not the same!" From that moment on, the pediatrician was no longer silent about his new-found faith.

The simple gospel, first presented through your personal testimony, then through a clear presentation such as the *Four Spiritual Laws,* is an extremely effective method of introducing others to Jesus. Let me give you a way to write your testimony so that nonbelievers can readily understand God's work in your life.

Preparation Guidelines

Your own testimony will be a natural introduction to sharing the gospel of Christ. A personal story opens listeners' hearts to hear more. Let God use your experiences to show people His light in you.

As you prepare to write your testimony, think through these six basic steps:

1. *Let God be original in you.* As you allow Him to work in and through you, He will use your unique personality and

situation to glorify Him. Don't expect your story to be like anyone else's. Let it be your own. Be yourself.

2. *Focus on Jesus Christ, not on your strengths.* Paul said he wanted to know nothing except Jesus Christ. When we put our focus on Christ and His life, death, burial, and resurrection, and on how He has transformed our lives, nonbelievers will see His love and forgiveness rather than our talents and abilities.

3. *Ask God to give you insight into how He has worked in your life.* Sometimes we don't recognize the greatest things God does. We may be too close to the situation to see how He has enabled us to grow in our faith. Ask Him to reveal what He has done in your life. Then use that insight to write your story.

4. *Concentrate on sharing with one person.* Many first-time speakers make the mistake of speaking to a group instead of to an individual. But if you write as though you are talking to one person, your testimony will be more direct. Each person in your audience will feel that you are sitting beside him or her personally to share your life.

5. *As you write, avoid Christian terminology.* Have you ever listened to a talk or a sermon where the speaker used such technical language that you got tired of listening or just couldn't understand? Try putting yourself into a non-Christian's shoes. He or she may not understand what "being saved" means or how to "ask Jesus into your heart." Use the same words in your testimony that you would use in a conversation with a nonbeliever or explain terms your audience may not comprehend. Your goal is to communicate with the nonbeliever.

6. *Read Acts 22, 23, and 26 and notice how Paul uses the "before/how/after" outline.* Use his example to guide you as you write your testimony. Remember these tips:

Be specific. Use direct language and clear illustrations. Describe details—within reason. Your testimony is not a biography of your life from childhood, so spend a brief time on the Before section. Limit your testimony to a five-minute presentation.

Be practical. Describe how God is helping you learn to trust Him more. Give examples, ways you have changed, or principles you have discovered in God's Word, and tell how you've applied them in your daily life.

Be realistic. Don't present your new life as problem-free or like living above the clouds. People want to hear how Christ has helped you through tough times and enabled you to solve difficult problems.

Perhaps you received Christ at an early age. Let me encourage you: A personal testimony is not simply a story of how God rescued someone from a life of horrible sin. It is an account of how God transforms lives—no matter where the person comes from or what circumstances the person has experienced. Many people are encouraged by the testimony of someone who was introduced to the Lord at an early age and who then avoided the many pitfalls of growing up. God uses each of us as we are, created in His image and transformed by His power.

One of my close friends, Doris Berven, told me that she didn't remember when she received Christ. She had been reared in a Christian home and heard about God's love and forgiveness from the time she could understand. I asked her, "What could you say?"

She responded, "I know that Christ is in my life, but I don't know when it happened!"

We agreed that the fact of knowing Christ is more important than being aware of when we came to know Him or how. Her testimony is a powerful one that she has shared with many.

In the Resources section, Vonette and I have provided three worksheets for your convenience: "Personal Testimony Preparation Guidelines," two "Personal Testimony Worksheets" (one for those who received Christ as an adult and one for those who have known Christ since childhood), and a "Personal Testimony Evaluation" form. You may use these as you prepare a basic outline of your testimony.

In the following pages, we have included three testimonies that follow the before/how/after outline. I'd like to begin with my testimony.

My Testimony

(Before)

The word *shy* describes me as a child. Even as an adult I was still shy, but most people thought of me as sophisticated. Underneath, though, I was fearful and uncomfortable—an angry, uptight, tense woman.

I married Howard Ball, an outgoing, loving man who helped me meet people. In time, we had two lovely children, Robbyn and Bob. Yet I still hadn't conquered my shyness, which caused me to live a self-centered life. I needed someone to rescue me from the bondage of myself.

(How)

A good friend, Gloria Miller, often talked to me about the peace of God through Jesus Christ. One day she invited me to a Bible study. I was apprehensive at first, but finally said, "Yes, I'll go with you."

Gloria reserved two seats in the front row. The teacher, who was standing right in front of me, said, "Everything I teach will be taken from the Scripture. Follow along as I read some Bible verses."

I attempted to follow along, but got lost. I knew nothing about that mysterious book. If the teacher had given a prize for the largest Bible, I would have won because I had brought our family Bible from our coffee table. Gloria offered to help me, but I was too embarrassed to admit my ignorance. I couldn't wait to leave, and determined never to return.

(Pertinent verse)

But the next week, I came again. Today I know that the prayers of my grandfather and mother and Gloria opened my heart. The message in John 14:6, "I am the way and the truth and the life. No one comes to the Father except through Me," revived my childhood memories and took root in my heart. I wanted to know the way and the truth and to change my life.

On the last night of that Bible study, I released my need and will to Jesus and He came into my life. I don't remember what I said, but I agreed with the leader's prayer asking for God's love and forgiveness.

(After)

Slowly, God released me from my bondage of shyness. I began enjoying people, inviting them to our home, finding it comfortable to converse. I began to relax and enjoy my wonderful family. And I'm still in the process of growing to be like Christ. Miles Stanford said, "It takes God a hundred years to make a good solid oak and only six months to make a squash." I don't want to be a squash.

I remember Gloria sharing with me that receiving Christ was the greatest experience a person could ever have. Once I made that decision, the process of change began. The life I always wanted—to be released from the bondage of myself—was mine through Christ's power.

Jared Billing's Testimony

(Before)

During the '30s, '40s and '50s, I had the good fortune of growing up in Miami, Florida, when it was still considered a medium-sized town. It was beautiful and clean, and a wonderful place to live. I was the last of three children, with a challenging older brother who was a good role model and an adoring older sister. We were a typical middle-class, hardworking, American family. Because our country was on the rebound from the depression and the second world war, the flourishing, positive atmosphere provided great opportunities for growth and success.

Since we went to Sunday school and church every Sunday, most people viewed us as a "Christian" family. I played football and basketball at Miami High School—a school with great tradition and undefeated records second to none in the country. My high school years were a great time of learning and success. I enjoyed everything about those years.

After graduation, I attended the University of Florida on a basketball scholarship and later graduated from the University of Miami with a business and law degree. I married the prettiest, most wonderful girl I had ever met, had three terrific children, and became a partner in a prestigious law firm. Soon, I was enjoying great success as a lawyer.

As I climbed the ladder of success—earning a lot of money, and enjoying a beautiful home, a wonderful family, and some professional recognition—I began wondering, *Is this all there is to life?* I became disillusioned and began searching for real meaning by reading philosophy books and attending life-enrichment seminars. During my search for truth, I read that there is a God-shaped vacuum in every person that only God can fill. Suddenly, I realized I was trying to put square pegs into round holes in my life. Even the greatest achievements, by the world's standards, could never satisfy the deepest longing of my heart.

(How)

Soon after, I attended a weekend retreat where I learned that God loved me and had a wonderful plan for my life. Frankly, I had never thought about consulting God about my state of affairs. But I found out that I was a sinful human and separated from God, therefore I was unable to know and experience His love and plan for me.

But God had made a provision for my delivery from sin by sending His Son, the Lord Jesus Christ, to pay my penalty for my sins. Growing up, I had learned this fact but had thought that attending church regularly and even teaching Sunday school satisfied all God's requirements for a relationship with Him. At the retreat, I understood that old adage: Regular church attendance no more makes you a Christian than standing in a garage makes you a car. Although I thought

I was a Christian, I was not. Instead, I had to personally invite Jesus into my life as a conscious decision of my mind and a definite act of my will. So I asked Jesus Christ to be my Savior, and He brought me *new* life.

(After)

Since Christ has come into my life, I have experienced many exciting changes. At first, I tried doing and not doing things that I thought would please God. Then I learned that He was not interested in cleaning up my old life. None of my own efforts to "improve" myself would succeed. My righteousness was no more than filthy rags and a parade of contrived, legalistic behavior that did not please God or satisfy my soul. Instead, Christ gave me new life and the power to grow in my faith. Christ came to live His life in and through me. Nothing else would do.

(Pertinent verse)

I discovered that spiritual growth is a lifetime experience involving my mind and my will. I think of my mind as a computer. The computer world recognizes the principle of "garbage in, garbage out." I had input years of wrong information and learning into my mind that had to be deprogrammed by allowing the mind of Christ to be formed in me through studying the Bible. Over the years, I also have painfully realized that I am not my own, but have been bought with a great price, the death of the Lord Jesus. As the apostle Paul writes in Colossians 1:27, "God has chosen to make known among the Gentiles the glorious riches of this mystery, which is Christ in you, the hope of glory."

The wonderful, overwhelming good news is that I have been given a new life—His life, which is reproduced in me by God's Holy Spirit. Now God's great gifts of mercy and compassion continue to complete the good work in me that He has begun! Thank you God, amen!

Kitty Oliver's Testimony

(Before)

I was raised in a Christian home by wonderful Christian parents and attended Christian schools. One Easter morning when I was about 10, I sat next to my parents in the fifth row of our church in St. Petersburg, Florida. Instead of drawing little pictures on my bulletin, I began listening to the pastor explain how Jesus Christ died on the cross for our sins. I felt as if the Lord said to me, "I died for you. I am your Father; you are my child. I love you." Suddenly, I understood what Jesus' death and resurrection meant! I wanted to go to heaven and be with Jesus. So I received Christ as my Savior that morning.

Years later, I graduated from college and began a career in fashion merchandizing. I started modeling professionally and eventually went into retailing. It was an exciting world with lots of attention, glamour, and lights. I began traveling and doing magazine work. Eventually, I became fashion director for Robinson's, a major department store.

Because of my career field, I was around many non-Christians who began to influence me. I pulled away from my Christian upbringing, and soon the peace that I had began leaving my life.

Eventually, I became engaged to a man who wasn't interested in spiritual things. In the middle of that engagement, I felt an absolute lack of peace. The Lord wouldn't allow me to be comfortable with my upcoming marriage.

(How)

After breaking the engagement, I decided to get away for a weekend to sort out what had been going on. My sister and brother-in-law, who lived in Miami, were planning a trip. I said, "Why don't I take care of your children so you can be alone?" That Saturday night, I was the only adult in their house. I felt so empty that I got down on my knees and cried out to God, "I can't stand the way I'm living. I want to live my life for You."

I got my nieces and nephew ready the next morning and went to the church that my sister and her family attended. I drove into the church parking lot, put the kids in the nursery, and sat in the front row of the sanctuary.

As I listened to the sermon, I longed to hear something to give me peace. The pastor described how much God loves us no matter what we do. At that point, I knew that the only way for me to live my life and be happy was to live it for Him. Right there, I made a decision to change the direction of my life.

(After)

I relocated to Miami and became statewide corporate fashion director for all Jordan March stores in Florida. I also began attending Bible studies in the community and at the church. Since the church I was attending had no singles' ministry, two friends went with me to the pastor, and we got his okay to start one.

Our first meeting included six singles. David Oliver, my future husband, taught the group. Over a period of months, the Bible study grew from six people to 120.

In time, David and I married. He's a wonderful, loving Christian husband, and we had dreams of a house full of children. Eight years later, we still had none. Because of my longing for children and my inability to have them, I went through a time of rebellion against the Lord.

But He just wouldn't let me go. Through my mistakes, grief, and confusion, He slowly and persistently drew me to Him. Finally, I hit rock bottom. Nothing could comfort me, so I cried out to Jesus, "If we never have children, You are all that matters. All I really want to do is live my life for You. If it means never having children, I give my desires to You. You are more important to me than children." For the first time, I really let go of the control of my life. I wanted to be an empty vessel that only He could fill.

Within six months, through God's love and compassion, we adopted a healthy, beautiful baby boy. He is the joy of our lives and has brought us more love than we ever thought possible.

Today David and I are involved in a lot of ministries. We have a Bible study in our home and I am involved in Women Today, a Campus Crusade ministry, and serve as chaplain of my tennis team.

As I look back, my life has been a journey with God. It began when I received Jesus as my Savior as a child. I changed directions when I heard that sermon in Miami. But the great turning point was when I fell on my knees, empty and unhappy, because David and I had no children. I had reached a low point emotionally but this was the high point in my spiritual journey. All that really mattered to me was Jesus Christ and living for Him.

I'm not saying that once you commit yourself to Jesus you get all of your wishes. He's not a Santa Claus. The spiritual journey is a growing process. As you get to know Jesus better, you want to please Him more. You love Him in a greater and deeper way, and He blesses you.

(Pertinent verse)

A verse that describes my journey with God is "No eye has seen, no ear has heard, no mind has conceived what God has prepared for those who love him" (1 Corinthians 2:9). That's exactly how God has worked in my life.

Getting Started

Now that you have read these testimonies, you can begin writing your own story. Read over the worksheets we have included to help you (listed on the following page). Practice giving your testimony before friends. Once you are satisfied that it is the way you want it, you can begin preparing to give a talk during a life-sharing event. Our next chapter will show you how to use your personal testimony as the foundation for your talk.

Included in the Resources for Effective Life Sharing

* Personal Testimony Preparation Guidelines
* Personal Testimony Worksheets
* Personal Testimony Evaluation

CHAPTER 12

Giving Your Personal Testimony

Vonette

SOME TIME ago, I related my personal testimony as part of my talk to a group of women in Oklahoma. Giving a clear presentation of the gospel, I challenged the women to invite Christ into their lives.

After I finished speaking, a woman came rushing up to me. "I finally understand what people have been bringing me to hear!" she exclaimed. "You explained so clearly how to become a Christian that I prayed the prayer and invited Jesus into my life."

As we talked, I discovered that she had been invited to a number of Christian functions by friends who wanted her to hear the good news of Jesus Christ. But she had never found spiritual answers to any of her questions. When someone invited her to this meeting, she agreed to come—but decided that it would be the last Christian event she would attend.

How tragic if we make opportunities for people to hear about Jesus, then do not clearly explain the gospel! That is why as Campus Crusade staff, we determined years ago that when we speak, we would always present the gospel simply and give an opportunity for people to receive Christ as their Savior.

To inspire an audience is not enough. We need to lead them to a place of commitment to Christ and help them by giving specific direction on how to do so. That's the challenge and excitement of speaking at life-sharing events. Your personal testimony and an explanation of how to become a child of God can help people enter the kingdom of heaven!

Before you answer, "But I can't speak. I've never done anything like that and would freeze," let me encourage you to examine the resources you have. In the previous chapter, you learned how to prepare your personal testimony. Here, you will find out how easy it is to turn your testimony into a 20- to 30-minute message.

God isn't looking for polished speakers. He uses Christians who simply make themselves available to Him and have a desire to help change lives. So before you close your mind to the possibility of speaking at a life-sharing event, ask God what He wants you to do.

As the Lord said to Moses, "Who has made man's mouth? Or who makes him dumb or deaf, or seeing or blind? Is it not I, the Lord? Now then go, and I, even I, will be with your mouth, and teach you what you are to say" (Exodus 4:11,12, NASB).

Jesus instructed His disciples, "It is not you who speak, but it is the Spirit of your Father who speaks in you" (Matthew 10:20, NASB).

Once you have decided that God wants you to give a talk, the first step is to prepare your message.

Preparing Your Message

The first thing I do to prepare is *ask God to cleanse me from any unknown sin*. I want to be a clean vessel for His use. I encourage you to claim Psalm 139:23,24 and ask God to reveal any sin in your life. Then confess the sins that He brings to mind and receive His forgiveness.

Second, once I have cleared my sin accounts with God, I *ask the Lord to fill me with His Holy Spirit*. I do not want any barrier to come between me and another person or to be a hindrance to someone who is open to receiving Christ. Therefore, I ask God to fill me with His Spirit as commanded in Ephesians 5:18. This gives me power to speak for His glory rather than my own.

Third, *I imagine the kinds of people who will attend.* What are their needs? Their backgrounds? Our common interests?

I ask, "Lord, what do you want me to say to these people? How can I give my testimony in a way that will touch their hearts?" Although my basic testimony remains the same, the way I tell it and the points I emphasize make it different each time I speak. I do not want my testimony to ever sound stale, so I ask God to make my talk fresh for that group.

Then I write out what I will say. I encourage you to put down your talk word-for-word, especially if this is the first time you have addressed a group. That way you can memorize it, then outline it or make notes to use during your presentation.

The following example of my talk gives step-by-step instructions on how to write yours. Included in the Resources is a "Speaker's Worksheet" that you can use to complete your first draft. Use the worksheet as you follow along with my example.

My Spiritual Journey

(Acknowledge the introduction that was given about you.)

I'm so glad to be here today. I want to thank (_____) for inviting me to speak."

(Identify with the listeners.)

As I look across the audience, I can't help but think, "I'd love to chat with each one of you to hear your life story. *You,* as a woman, are significant. You have something to offer."

(Give a humorous story or interesting comment to relax your audience.)

I love being a woman. And God loves us just as we are. When He created the world, He did it in seven days. After each day's work, He said, "That's good." Then He created man. But He said, "I can do better than that." So He created woman.

He created her last, not because she is best, but so she wouldn't tell Him how to create everything else.

(Use the title of the message as an introduction to your testimony. These remarks should set the audience at ease and prepare them for the topic.)

Since we represent a variety of generations in this room, we've all had different experiences. I've been asked to share how my experiences have shaped my spiritual journey and how God has worked in my life.

(Share your personal testimony:)

I grew up in a small town in Oklahoma called Coweta. My childhood years were spent during one of the most secure times in history. As a child, I knew I was loved. The community was small, and everyone participated in rearing the children.

(Before)

Church was a vital part of community life. Every time the doors opened, I was there. Yet, it wasn't until later that God became a reality in my life.

After graduating from high school, I attended Texas Women's University. It was there that I first questioned what I believed and why. Was my faith that of my parents or did it mean something to me? As I read the Bible, it was just so many words on the page.

Minoring in a difficult subject, chemistry, I needed as much help as possible. The group I wanted to study with met on Sunday mornings. That forced me to analyze why I went to church. Was it merely because I enjoyed the music? In fact, I had a hard time concentrating on the sermon. Many times, I found myself looking at women's hats during the service. My hobby was watercolor, so I would note the percentage of reds and yellows and other interesting details.

Then a young man walked into my life. He was handsome, successful, and moral—and had grown up in Coweta, too. But now he lived in southern California. One day he wandered into Hollywood Presbyterian Church and committed his life to

Christ. He remembered how active I had been in our church back in Oklahoma, so he thought I might be interested in what had happened to him. I was, but I was more interested in him than in what he had to say.

Bill Bright and I corresponded for a number of months. Every week, I received flowers, candy, a telegram, or a telephone call. He was so creative in his letters that it was fun to hear from him. Since he owned his own confectionery business, he had more resources than the average college man, and I became famous on campus as the girl who dated the candy man.

He traveled to the campus to escort me to the spring Red Bud Ball, the big event of the season. And he proposed to me on our first date. Over the weekend, I realized that I was in love with Bill. He was everything I could ask for in a husband. So I said yes. Later, he went to Oklahoma to ask my mother and father for my hand. They were pleased with Bill but encouraged us to wait until I had earned my degree before we married. We agreed.

While we were apart, Bill was growing in his faith. At the same time, I was getting farther and farther away from mine. Finally, I came to the conclusion that Bill was being influenced by a group of fanatical people in California and needed to be rescued. We couldn't possibly be married unless he became more "reasonable" in his religious ideas.

(How)

After my graduation, Bill invited me to attend a college ministry conference in California. I was surprised at what I found there. I met a thousand young people from all over the United States who were sharp and attractive, knew where they were going, and how they were getting there. They talked about their faith as if God was real in their lives.

I listened carefully to what they had to say, wishing I could possess the quality of life they had. But I decided what they had wasn't real, and eventually they would return to normal.

I really loved Bill Bright. But I decided that this relationship would not work out for me. The best thing we could do was break our engagement.

Concerned, Bill suggested that I talk with Dr. Henrietta Mears, who had taught chemistry in the Minneapolis schools and was now director of Christian education at the Hollywood Presbyterian Church. Dr. Mears knew that Bill and I were engaged, and she had been praying for me for months.

She immediately asked me if I had received Christ as my Savior. "Oh, yes," I replied. "I joined the church at ten years of age and attended church camp every year in high school. But God is not real to me. I'm not sure that He could be to anyone."

Miss Mears explained that God loves me and has a wonderful plan for my life. She told me, "Christ said, 'I have come that you might have life and have it more abundantly.'"

I remember thinking, *If God has a plan for my life, I wish He would hurry up and tell me what it is.*

Then she explained that the reason we can't know God's love and plan for our lives is because of our sin. I remember thinking, *Please, speak for yourself. I'm not a sinner. I have worked at being a good girl. I'll match my morals with anyone.*

Then Miss Mears went on to say that sin was falling short of the glory of God. We all have to admit that we can never achieve perfection and that, try as we may, we fall short of God's standard. Since that is true in all of our lives, a term had to be coined to describe this condition. That word is sin.

Dr. Mears went on to share Romans 6:23, which says that the wages of sin is death, a spiritual separation from God, but the gift of God is eternal life through Jesus Christ our Lord.

Well, if Christ is the way to eternal life, how do we have Him? Dr. Mears read John 14:6 where Jesus says, "I am the way and the truth and the life. No one comes to the Father except through me."

"It isn't enough to believe in God," she said. "We must receive Christ individually. In Revelation 3:20, Jesus says He stands at the door and knocks. This means the door of our hearts, emotions, will, and intellect. The verse goes on to say that if anyone opens the door to Him, He will come in."

(After)

She challenged me that day to perform an experiment. "Let's just enter God's laboratory. You may have received Christ before, but you want to make sure that you've done it. Let's apply the formula that I shared with you. Invite Jesus to come into your heart and see what happens."

(Relate two practical illustrations of ways God has worked in your life. Make clear that Christ made the difference, not circumstances or hard work.)

That's what I did. I applied the principles that God loves me, that I was separated from Him, that Jesus was the way to God, the Father, and that I needed to receive Him. I asked Jesus to come into my life and forgive my sins, to make me the person He wants me to be.

That is when my life began to change. I learned that it does not matter when you receive Christ—as a child, a young adult, a middle-age person, or a senior adult. You cannot grow in your faith until you are sure that Christ is in your life. When you begin to trust Him, adhere to Him, and believe in Him, He begins to reveal Himself to you.

The first thing that happened was that my prayers began to go beyond the ceiling. I felt they were being heard. And my Bible became a living book to me.

I began to see God directing my steps. Now Bill and I were in agreement. We had a confirmation that we were to marry. After the wedding, we began to apply our faith to our relationship. As God led us, we began to accomplish more than I ever dreamed we could. We saw many people introduced to the Lord through the teams Bill led that went to jails, road camps, hospitals, and skid-row missions. As we ministered at these places, he realized that no one was going to the college campuses. The Lord led Bill (and me) to start a ministry called Campus Crusade for Christ. And what a privilege it has been over the past forty-five years to see what God chooses to do through staff members who are committed to reaching people for His kingdom.

(Make a transition to the Four Spiritual Laws.*)*

What Miss Mears shared with me that day is found in this little booklet called the *Four Spiritual Laws.* I would like to give each of you a copy, then go through it with you, so that you too can understand the simple truths I discovered that day.

The illustrations you give will help your listeners understand what God has done in your life. Always remember that you may be talking to non-Christians. Therefore, keep the language simple and free from Christian terms. Let the illustrations give insights into how you felt, thought, and reacted in situations.

Give specific information, and answer such questions as: Why did I become angry? How did I react? What did I do about it? The more people can see, hear, touch, taste, and smell in your illustrations, the more they will relate to what you are saying.

The most important point to emphasize is that Christ made the difference in your life. Otherwise, it appears as if you have been responsible for the changes in your life. Non-Christians need to hear that not only must Christ be *in* your life, He must also *control* your life for you to live above your circumstances and in His joy.

And be realistic. Christians are not perfect. Your audience will learn how to handle their own sin by observing how you managed yours. Avoid speaking on a spiritual plane that no one can hope to reach. Tell what can happen in everyday situations to a person who allows God to lead and control his or her life.

When you finish writing your talk, practice giving it until you feel comfortable with what you will present. You may want to practice in front of Christian friends for suggestions on how to make your message more effective.

We have found it most convenient for the person giving the talk to also present the gospel as a part of his or her message. Barbara and I recommend using the *Four Spiritual Laws*, a concise way to make God's plan of salvation clear to nonbelievers. The Resources include a section on "How to Present the *Four Spiritual Laws*" that gives more detail on how to use the booklet in a gospel presentation. Also note the worksheet entitled "Outline for Your Talk," which you can take with you to help you stay on track during your message.

Writing Your Biography

Whenever you speak at a life-sharing event, the host needs to know how to introduce you to the group. It is helpful to him or her if you prepare something in advance. A biography (bio for short) is a few statements about yourself, such as where you were born; where you went to school; where you work; and, if you are married, information about your spouse and children. Include any special recognition and accomplishments that relate to your topic.

The purpose of your bio is to help your audience identify with you and to put them at ease. Therefore, be specific and informal in what you include. A touch of humor is effective if it can be presented naturally. Give your bio to the person who will introduce you. Encourage the host or hostess to include only information that relates to your audience. If you feel a little uncomfortable after being introduced, you may respond with humor such as, "After that introduction, I can hardly wait to hear what I'm going to say!"

Giving Your Message

The day of the event, arrive a half hour early at the home where you will speak. Offer to help the host finish last-minute preparations and pray together as a team. Then be available to the host as he or she greets the guests.

After the host introduces you, begin your talk. Give each person a *Four Spiritual Laws* booklet and read through it as they follow along. When you get to the prayer on page 10, read it and the question and statement immediately following. Invite listeners who want to receive Christ to pray silently as you read the prayer again, phrase by phrase. You might say something like this: "For many of you, this prayer will express the desire of your heart. If you are not sure that Christ is in your life, let me suggest that you pray this prayer to be sure. Pray silently as I pray aloud. Let's pray." Read the prayer slowly. Then finish going through the booklet with your audience.

After you have read through the *Four Spiritual Laws*, hand out 3×5 cards and pencils and ask your guests to write the following:

* Their name, address, and phone number
* Any comments or questions they have
* An "X" beside their name if they invited Christ into their life for the first time

Ask your guests to fold their cards in half and leave them in a convenient location, such as a basket set out on a table. Thank the host and turn the meeting over to him or her. Then make yourself available to visit with guests. When you initiate conversations with guests, others will do the same.

Here is this same information summarized in a simple outline you can follow:

* Thank the host for inviting you to speak.
* Establish rapport with your audience.
* Give your personal testimony.
* Transition to the *Four Spiritual Laws*.
* Present the gospel by using the booklet.
* Give an invitation to receive Christ through prayer.
* Pray.
* Ask everyone to fill out a comment card.
* Thank the host and turn the meeting over to him or her.

Conversations After Your Talk

After the meeting, you will find many opportunities to share personally with members of your audience. Train yourself to be lovingly direct. Ask the question: "Did you pray that prayer with me today?" Depending on the response, you may be able to assure a person that he or she is a Christian, make an appointment for later, or take time right then to talk. Some non-Christians may have objections or may have erected barriers to the gospel. Let me share several things you can do when counseling others about their spiritual needs.

Guide the conversation toward Christ. Many people will have questions or make comments that do not relate to their spiritual needs. You can naturally turn a conversation toward Christ. Use these tips as a guide.

- **Love others genuinely**. People sense how others feel about them. If you are answering questions out of obligation, he or she may turn cold in a hurry. Instead, view that person as a unique part of God's creation and of priceless worth to our Lord, which is absolutely true.

- **Establish rapport**. You have begun this process through your talk. Now turn your heart toward the individual's needs and concerns. It will take only a few minutes to express your care and concern, but it can open that person's heart to hear what you say.

- **Talk about Jesus**. Many people will have legitimate questions about different religions or denominations, or other related issues. But avoid letting yourself get sidetracked with these topics. The central concern is Jesus Christ and our relationship with Him. Keep directing the conversation back to Jesus and what He has done for us.

- **Use stories**. Although people are interested in ideas, they relate more to personal experiences. The word "witness" actually means to give a first-person account. Tell the true story of how Christ has worked in your life.

Some people may raise objections during your conversation, such as: "I don't believe the Bible," "I've seen too many hypocrites," "I'm not ready to make such a commitment," "I have my own religion; I don't need anything more," and so on.

Do not be afraid of these objections. By seeking you out, the person has indicated a desire to know Christ. But he or she may be trying to work through unresolved questions. Instead of arguing about peripheral points, bring that person back to your testimony and how you know for sure that Christ is in your life. If the non-Christian does not seem ready to receive Christ, do not push. Try to determine if the objection is coming from a misunderstanding or a hurt suffered in the past. Then encourage that person to reread the *Four Spiritual Laws* booklet at home and to receive Christ by praying the prayer in the booklet. Make yourself available to talk to this individual at a later date.

You may encounter someone who seems hostile to the gospel. Many times this attitude is only a smoke screen that hides a deep desire for God. If this should happen, never argue with the person. Instead, reason within the listener's expertise. For example, if the person you are counseling is a teacher, show how Jesus taught His disciples about God.

And *never let someone's initial resistance discourage you*. Be patient. Remember that success in witnessing is simply taking the initiative to share Christ in the power of the Holy Spirit and leaving the results to God.

Paul writes, "Devote yourselves to prayer, being watchful and thankful. And pray for us, too, that God may open a door for our message, so that we may proclaim the mystery of Christ, for which I am in chains. Pray that I may proclaim it clearly, as I should" (Colossians 4:2–4). That's my prayer for you: that your speaking ministry will result in many finding Christ as their Savior and growing in their faith. Nothing brings more joy and satisfaction.

Included in the Resources for Effective Life Sharing

* Speaker's Worksheet
* How to Present the *Four Spiritual Laws*

Special Events

*By adapting the basic life-sharing
format, you can use your home to
host children's and youth gatherings,
video events, Christmas celebrations,
and to reach out into the community.*

CHAPTER 13

Reaching Out to the Community

Barbara

AS I BEGAN to host life-sharing events, I naturally wanted to reach out in my community to friends I had met through civic involvement. I worked with Child Help, U.S.A., a home for battered and abused children in the southern California desert, and with the Inland Empire Symphony. When I asked four Christian friends to join me as co-hosts, they eagerly agreed. We met, prayed, and planned, and we named our group "New Beginning." A couple of the women were members of the country club, so we scheduled our first party there.

While working at Child Help, I had met June Haver McMurray. She had been a Hollywood star during the '40s, and had married the well-known actor Fred McMurray. I was drawn to June's warm, compassionate heart for God.

As a group, we had a brilliant idea. Why not ask June to speak at our event? But when I called to ask her, she said, "Oh, no. I don't do that." Although she was very gracious, she was also very firm!

Two days later, she called me back. "I heard Billy Graham on television," she said, "and when he closed his message, he gave a call for Christians to witness for their Lord. I just knew he was talking to me. So I'll come."

When my friends learned about June's call, they were excited. We planned to meet at 10:30 a.m., have June speak for an hour, then eat lunch. So we prayed and sent out our invitations.

The response was great! June shared her life story beautifully and lovingly. Since childhood days, she had wanted to become a nun. Then she met Fred McMurray and in the process had come to know Jesus Christ as her Savior. Now she was growing in her faith.

After twenty-five minutes, she concluded her talk. We had planned for an hour, so I discreetly asked her if she would share some more. "No," she replied, "that's all I have to say."

I could see that the women were waiting to hear more, so I suggested, "Why don't you answer questions from the audience."

"Oh, no," she insisted. "Why don't I ask them questions instead?"

My first thought was, *This won't work,* but we went ahead and tried it anyway.

She began asking the women for ideas on how to reach her grown children for Christ. June's question touched a soft nerve in Peggy's heart, a woman who had grown children herself. She stood up and said in a trembling voice, "I grew up in a Christian home, but resented going to church every Sunday morning and evening and Wednesday night. So when I was in college, I decided to marry an atheist or an agnostic so I wouldn't have to go to church. Eventually, I married a successful attorney, and we now have two beautiful girls.

"What you said this morning stirred the memories of my parents' faith. Now I know how my waywardness made them feel.

"I know that somewhere in the Bible it says that faith comes from hearing the Word of God. From what I've heard today, I think I still have my faith."

June exclaimed, "Honey! You have got it!"

Everyone laughed. I saw God using humor with truth to give Peggy assurance that she could restore her relationship with God.

An Emerging Ministry

What fun we had in New Beginning! We invited many speakers, some even well known, such as Dr. Henry Brandt, a Christian psychologist, author, and speaker; Emily Barnes, an author and speaker; and Bobbe Evans, the wife of Miami Dolphin player Norm Evans.

One day, Howard and I decided it would be great if husbands and wives came together to hear couples share their testimonies. We prayed, then planned a Saturday brunch at the country club. We invited Bill and Sally Kanaga to share about their marriage. Bill was formerly the president and chairman of the Arthur Young Accounting Firm and national president of the Chamber of Commerce.

Bill and Sally did such a good job. They related how they had opened their lives to Christ and how He was helping them with their marriage, family, and personal relationships. Howard and I continued to host these brunches two or three times a year. As a result, many people received Christ as their Savior.

Eventually I became the chaplain, then president of our local Child Help chapter, which raised funds for the children's village. Through the organization, I met new friends from many religious backgrounds who had good hearts and wanted to help children. Then I hosted an event in which a young Christian woman, the wife of an NFL football player, shared with us about her abusive years in a difficult home. She described how she had learned of God's love for her. Those of us in Child Help who knew the Lord continued to make the most of our opportunities by listening, loving, and sharing with others.

As I have found, evangelistic entertaining works well outside the neighborhood. People everywhere are hungry for a personal, loving relationship. Just as your neighborhood can be a base for a home ministry, you can also invite friends you meet at work, at social events, or at secular organizations into your ministry circle.

Steps to Reaching Your Community

The secret to reaching your community is to *get involved*. Many times, our lives become so busy with family and church activities that we eliminate everything else. But our community needs a dynamic Christian influence. Without neglecting your church involvement, I encourage you to seek out organizations you can join, such as sports clubs, music groups, career associations, employee or employer meetings, craft circles, local government groups, or charity organizations. Your natural interests can lead to evangelistic opportunities. Also, remember to use the contacts you already have to expand your ministry of life sharing.

Once you have decided where you fit in, *be friendly, loving, and caring* to those with whom you work and those in your community. This includes having more than a one-subject interest in people; it means also asking them about their families, their hopes and dreams, and their problems. Life sharing gets involved with lives, rather than just with projects and committees.

Then begin to *pray for those you have met*. Ask God to give you creative ideas for reaching them with His love and forgiveness and to give you wisdom in how to get involved in their lives, using your home to introduce them to Christ.

Sometimes simple friendship can get in the way of an open witness, so *be aggressive in seeking God and His ways to meet needs and present the gospel*. I'm tempted many times to stand back and let other people make the first introduction. But then I think of the example of the apostle Paul. He was bold; he went where people gathered, whether in the synagogue or down by the river. His primary goal was to share the new life he had found in Jesus Christ with as many nonbelievers as would listen. In Colossians 4:2–4, he prayed for opportunities to present the gospel clearly. Like Paul, we may need to pray for open doors to present the gospel.

God has placed you in a unique sphere of influence. Use what you have for His glory; let the sweet savor of the Holy Spirit permeate the lives of others no matter where you work or play. Following are a few examples of how you could host community events.

The Symphony

Let me share how I reached out through my involvement in the local symphony.

I was excited when I received an invitation to the first organizational meeting of a group of people who were interested in bringing a symphony to our community.

When the symphony became a reality, I was elected social vice president. What fun I had, planning pre-concert get-togethers and after-concert galas, and working with the most enjoyable people!

Through my involvement in the symphony, I made many new friends. I learned the value of being accountable and responsible and following through with the things I said I would do. I desired to let Jesus Christ live in me and do His will through me. To my great surprise and delight, people often sought me out because of my faith.

I invited members of the symphony to some of my life-sharing events. In fact, several members were present at the first brunch where Bill and Sally Kanaga gave a talk. We also included friends from Child Help and the Chamber of Commerce. Many left renewed in their faith or newly committed to solving their marriage difficulties, and some received Christ.

Jazzercise

At age 40, I decided to exercise! I'm certainly not the athletic type, but I needed to keep in shape. So I joined a Jazzercise group. The leader, Patty, was a fun-loving, energetic person. We became friends over lunch and Patty asked me if I would host a Bible study. She had heard I was a Christian and hoped I would help her share her faith with others. I considered this an opportunity from the Lord!

Sixteen of the women in our exercise group came to the Bible study. They were from various backgrounds and had different problems, such as divorce, blended marriages, challenging home situations, lesbian leanings, and so on. But they were open to looking into God's Word.

We met for a year, and all who attended either received Christ as their Savior or renewed their faith. Patty and I could never explain how that happened, but I watched as the women gave evidence of their new faith in their changed lives. Of course, we eventually expanded our outreach to include husbands and children, too. This ministry of life sharing has been one of the greatest privileges of my life.

Track Walking

I began track walking because I had dislocated my elbow during a fall while jogging and had a long recovery with therapy and a brace. I began walking around the local school track in the early morning and became friends with some of the dearest people. Howard named us the Dawn Patrol.

Sometimes they came for coffee after we walked. I hosted Christmas and Easter coffees (we all wore dressy walking clothes). Again, God brought some of these dear friends to Himself. For others, their understanding of Jesus was broadened, and we were all blessed as we fellowshiped together.

When they learned I was moving to Florida, my track-walking friends put on a party for me at the track. They made signs that said nice things and placed them around the track so that I could read them on my walk. And they brought delicious food. What fun!

God has shown me through incidents like these that this shy person who once was afraid of people now loves to reach out. I can enjoy every person God brings my way.

Lunch With a Friend

I look for opportunities to share my faith with people at every activity. I enjoy asking just one new friend to come to my house for lunch. Large group events are meaningful and fun, but wonderful conversations can result from one-to-one relationships.

After joining the PTA at our local school, I was introduced to the president. Mary had an enjoyable personality and created a happy atmosphere while leading the meetings, so I invited her to my home for lunch. First we went shopping, then we relaxed at my house.

After we ate, she asked me what Howard and I did for a living. I briefly related our testimony and how God had worked in our lives to allow us to be in ministry full-time. "The best explanation for what we believe," I continued, "is in a little booklet called the *Four Spiritual Laws.* Could I share it with you?"

She said, "Yes, I'd like that," so I began reading through the booklet. Upon reaching the part that describes two different kinds of people—those with self-directed lives and those with Christ-directed lives—I asked her, "Which circle represents your life?"

Mary quickly responded, "I'd really better get going." She thanked me for lunch, then informed me that she was active in her church and sang in the choir. Her voice sounded upset. She promptly picked up the *Four Spiritual Laws* and left.

As soon as the door closed behind her, I began to regret sharing with her. When Howard got home, I described what happened. "I'm afraid I got ahead of the Lord in my sharing."

Howard laughed. "I didn't know anyone could get ahead of the Lord."

We laughed together, then prayed for Mary. Even so, I woke up in the middle of the night worrying about what had happened. I prayed again, then fell asleep.

The next morning, Mary called. "When I got home yesterday," she exclaimed, "I read through that booklet again. I prayed and received Christ, and then read the booklet with my husband, Ken. He prayed, too!"

Excited, I invited them over for dinner. The four of us shared together about the love of Christ and what happens when a person receives Him as Savior and Lord.

Since then, Mary and Ken have been exceptional friends. Howard and I have seen them experience physical problems and a fire that destroyed their home, but they always lean heavily on the grace of God. They have helped us minister to many people over the years.

This is what can happen over lunch or dinner in your home—whether with a large crowd, a small group, or just one person. When we know how to share our faith, walk in the power of the Holy Spirit, and make ourselves available to be used by Him, what an exciting life we have as believers!

Opportunities in the Workplace

Today, witnessing in the workplace has become more of a challenge. But life sharing gives Christians another way to share their faith—through their home.

Let me first mention a few basic principles that can pave the way for your witness. First, *do your work heartily as unto the Lord*. Nothing mars a person's testimony like failure to be conscientious and hard-working. That doesn't mean that you have to succeed at everything you do. Most co-workers respect a colleague who does his or her job and maintains a positive attitude. Being pleasant during difficult situations will draw people to you. As Paul writes in Philippians 2:14,15, "In everything you do, stay away from complaining and arguing, so that no one can speak a word of blame against you. You are to live clean, innocent lives as children of God in a dark world full of people who are crooked and stubborn. Shine out among them like beacon lights, holding out to them the Word of Life" (TLB).

Second, *be careful what you say*. A Christian's witness can be harmed in the workplace through an uncontrolled tongue. If an employee criticizes co-workers behind their backs, his or her testimony will not glorify God. But the kind of Christian who shows love to others even when they are not present reflects the love of Christ.

Third, *be sensitive about using company time to talk to others about Christ*. Your employer is paying you to accomplish your work and has the right to expect good performance. You will, however, find natural opportunities to talk with others about your faith, such as during lunch breaks and before or after work.

Fourth, *invite your co-workers to your home for brunch or a dessert*. This allows your co-worker to relate with you in a more casual atmosphere and opens the door to subjects that he or she might not feel are appropriate to talk about during work hours. Begin by developing strong relationships with your colleagues, then invite those you know best to a life-sharing event in your home. Once one person in your office or workplace gets excited about life sharing, his or her enthusiasm will help you reach out to more co-workers with the gospel. In time, you may be able to begin a Bible study during lunch or before or after work. As God leads you, He will work in this sphere of influence just as He does in your neighborhood.

Fifth, *host a weekly luncheon for working women,* either where you work or in your neighborhood. Or schedule a once-a-month salad supper at one of the women's homes and encourage people to bring a guest for a sharing time. Make your program short so that your guests can get enough rest for the next day.

Large Events

As you become more experienced at hosting life-sharing events, you may want to be part of a large gathering. Such a dinner or party requires a team of people who can divide the responsibilities and arrangements. Betty Madison was involved in planning a large luncheon in Birmingham, Alabama, in which Vonette spoke and I gave my testimony. Betty explains how she and her committee hosted this event.

Betty

Emalee Newbold, Charlotte Brown, and I decided to plan a large women's brunch to reach community and state leaders for Christ. I spent lots of hours on the telephone. Everyone had a great time, but I had the most fun of all! Let me share with you what we did to plan and host our brunch, including the committees we set up and the responsibilities the committee members had.

Invitation Committee: Our first priority was to appoint an invitation chairman, who has the most time-consuming responsibility in working with the invitation list. Charlotte graciously accepted the position. Charlotte and I then approached other friends to serve on various committees and invited them to a luncheon where we discussed the brunch.

We bought a "Blue Book" of elected officials for the state of Alabama that included the names and addresses of supreme court justices, state judges, local and county judges, city commissioners, school board officials, county commissioners, presidents of local colleges and universities, and media celebrities. We invited female leaders and the wives of male leaders. The first day of January, we mailed the beautifully printed invitations requesting response by January 15, two weeks before the brunch date.

In most cases, we sent a note along with the invitation written by a person in the field of service. For instance, Mrs. Hugh Maddox, wife of a supreme court justice, invited the other justices' wives to come and sit at her table. A local judge's wife and county commissioner's wife invited the other county commissioners wives. These people were guests of the committee and were seated at the head table.

As we received the return cards, we evaluated the response, then told the hostesses how many personal friends they could invite to fill their tables. Although we filled all fifty tables, we did not begin to touch all of our community. The hostesses made it a point to invite non-Christians first, so we had a good representation of worldly and Spirit-filled Christians and non-Christian guests.

Facilities Committee: Two people agreed to handle all the arrangements at the country club, such as seating and menus.

In our brunch, we served five hundred people, so parking became an important issue. When you plan your brunch, don't forget to consider parking availability. Inadequate parking space can delay your program and cause frustration for your guests.

Decorating Committee: A woman who is known for exquisite decorating agreed to help us. She got a committee of six to help her plan and decorate the club. They did a grand job—the centerpieces were breathtakingly beautiful! At the conclusion of the brunch, the centerpieces were given to the table hostesses.

Prayer Committee: The chairwoman wrote out specific prayer requests, encouraged us in prayer the weeks before the event, and led us in prayer at the brunch. The prayer committee encouraged the hostesses to pray for the guests they would invite to the brunch. The chairwoman also volunteered to help me write follow-up letters and other correspondence.

Brunch Committee: We asked fourteen women to serve as brunch committee members. Each was requested to host a table of ten people and to ask additional people to host a table.

On the day of our event, we set numbers on the tables before guests arrived. Then we stationed two to four people at the door to direct guests to the right tables. We also placed name tags at each plate for guests to fill out, and had the hostesses' name tags prepared in calligraphy beforehand.

We held a drawing and gave a book as a prize to each table. Each hostess handled the drawing at her table. We had purchased fifty books, and also gave one to give each guest at the head table.

Finance Committee: One woman served as treasurer. She was in charge of the hostesses who sold tickets for their own tables. I sold tickets for about three tables to individuals who called because they had heard of our brunch by word of mouth. Each hostess invited her guests to sit with her at her table and gave them tickets with the table number printed on them. The hostess then brought one check for the total amount to the treasurer. That helped the treasurer because she didn't have so many checks to handle.

Since we were trying to keep the cost to a minimum, one of the committee members volunteered to buy Vonette's plane fare. Also, we planned a brunch rather than a lunch because it was cheaper and we didn't have to offer dessert. We served crepes, fruit, and beverage.

Program Committee: We kept the program to a minimum with the chairman serving as the matron of ceremonies. We had a welcome, an introduction of those at the head table, a prayer, a song, and Barbara Ball's five-minute personal testimony. Our soloist's song was powerful and beautiful. Then Vonette spoke approximately 40 minutes. At the close of her speech, she went through the *Four Spiritual Laws* booklet and discussed the comment card, a copy of which we had placed beside each plate.

Vonette was great, and the ladies were hungry for spiritual guidance. We received outstanding comments on the cards.

Follow-up Committee: During the brunch, twenty women indicated decisions to receive Christ and two wanted to know more about Jesus Christ. For example, a supreme court justice's wife and a county commissioner's wife checked the boxes on their card to indicate that they had received Christ. We also offered our guests an opportunity to join a Bible study, and received many requests for morning and evening Bible studies for women and for couples. On the comment cards, several asked that we also start a women's movement in Montgomery.

We learned that an essential to follow-up is pre-planning so the follow-up can begin immediately after the brunch. The hostesses continued in prayer for their guests, and in most cases, followed up on the women who sat at their table.

Media Committee: Since all guests were invited personally, we did not do any pre-brunch publicity. But our media chairman invited newspaper and television coverage to give greater exposure to God's work in our community. Vonette was shown on the evening news in an interview highlighting the brunch, and Saturday's religious page contained a review of the brunch. A local weekly social events paper covered the luncheon and named key ladies who hostessed and decorated.

Barbara

As you can see, hosting a large event takes preparation and a committee of dedicated, Spirit-filled Christians. But the influence you can have on your community has such far-reaching effects that the effort is well worth it.

If you sense that the Lord is leading you to organize a large dinner, party, or brunch, ask Christians to help you who have had experience in hosting a large gathering. I know you will be blessed by the results you see from your commitment to life sharing beyond your neighborhood—and you will have enjoyable experiences at the same time!

CHAPTER 14

Planning Exciting Children's Events

Vonette

YEARS AGO, Morris and Linda Erickson's two daughters, Tana and Tracy, often played in their yard with other children from their neighborhood. But some of the kids used bad language. Morris and Linda wondered what they could do to change the atmosphere while the children played and how they could reach the neighborhood children for Christ.

Morris and Linda started a Bible club in their home, and the neighborhood youngsters came to hear Bible stories each week. One day, Morris overheard several children discussing the families who lived in the neighborhood. One boy pointed to the Erickson house and said firmly, "Oh, they teach about Jesus there."

That comment impressed Morris. "There can be no greater compliment paid," he says, "than for a child to regard your home as a place where he learns about Jesus." That incident and other considerations led Morris and Linda into a lifetime of working with children. In 1974 Morris became a field director for the Northwest area of Child Evangelism Fellowship Inc. in North Dakota, and in 1994 he became the state director.

A neighborhood presents one of the most effective places for reaching children with the gospel. When Morris speaks to churches, he urges Christian families to use their home as a "mission station in the neighborhood."

Life Sharing With Children

When I was growing up in Coweta, our town was important to the residents, and children were the concern of the entire community. I remember an incident with Mr. Newton, who was a city lawyer and had been a college English professor. I took voice and art lessons from his wife. Beginning in fifth grade, I was in their home once or twice a week.

One afternoon, I arrived for a lesson and rang the doorbell. Mrs. Newton called out, "Who is it?"

"It's me, Vonette."

She asked me to wait outside until she had finished another pupil's lesson. Mr. Newton, who was sitting on the porch swing, invited me to join him. When I sat down, he began to give me a grammar lesson. "The proper reply is 'It is I,'" he said. We rehearsed several scenarios of using "I" and "me."

What does this incident have to do with life sharing? Mr. Newton took an interest in helping me grow. He was typical of many adults in Coweta who invested time in the children's lives.

Mother sponsored parties in our home so she would know where her children were and what we were doing, and so she could get acquainted with our friends. Other parents felt the same way. The interaction between adults and children enriched all of our lives.

Today, in most neighborhoods in which we live, children play next door or a few houses down the street. We have unprecedented opportunities to minister to these youngsters. Some are latchkey students with time on their hands; others need a good relationship with adults. We can show Christian love to these little ones and introduce them to the Person who will care for them no matter where they are or what situations they face.

Children's events can involve everyone. Many Christian households make them a family project. Some home-school parents incorporate children's parties and Bible clubs into their school activities.

Elementary children love to learn about God, and they don't require elaborate decorations or expensive activities. Instead, these youngsters enjoy listening to Bible stories.

Life sharing with children can benefit the entire family. As you open your home to them, your sons and daughters will get to know others their age on a spiritual basis, you will set a spiritual tone in your children's conversations. This will teach them to introduce their friends to Jesus. In the process, you will get better acquainted with your neighbors, and can share your faith with them too.

What's Involved?

Children's events are simple to plan and easy to host, and, with a little adjustment, can fit smoothly into your schedule. You may have parties as frequently as you like.

Monthly parties can follow a theme. Here are some suggested party ideas:

January—*Beginning a New Year With God*

February—*Valentines and God's Love*

March—*Spring Brings New Life*

April—*Easter Surprise, Jesus Is Alive!*

May—*School's Almost Out!*

June—*Summer's Here!*

July—*Picnic Party*

August—*Sonshine Day*

September—*Fall Fun Time*

October—*Harvest Party*

November—*Thanksgiving*

December—*Birthday Party for Jesus*

To plan your party or Bible club meeting, *begin with prayer*. You may want to ask several people to pray with you. List the names of the children you want to invite and begin praying specifically for them and their families.

Ask another adult to help you *plan your meeting* or to teach the Bible lesson if you prefer to serve as hostess. Asking a non-Christian neighbor to help host the event can expose that person to God's Word and ease his or her concerns about the event at the same time. Many people have received Christ as a result of observing children's faith and listening to the truth of God's Word at a party or club.

Then *select a place* to hold your event and *set a date* that will be convenient for everyone involved. Right after school is an excellent time for weekly or daily meetings. Saturdays or evenings work well for monthly parties. Prepare invitations with the time, date, and place of your meeting, as well as how often it will occur. Also, don't let neighbors find out from their children that you are teaching Bible stories. Instead, state the reason for the event on your invitation or speak to the parents directly so they won't misunderstand what you will be doing.

Now, *gather your material.* You will need a Bible story with visual aids that fits your event. A time-tested lesson is the Wordless Book. (Directions for making the book and teaching this lesson are in the Resources.) If you are planning five sessions, find a story that includes five lessons. For a holiday or theme party, choose a Bible lesson that fits the occasion. Also, purchase children's tracts like the children's *Four Spiritual Laws,* the *Good News Comic Book*, or the *Good News Glove* to help you introduce a child to Christ. Child Evangelism Fellowship and your local bookstore have a wealth of resources available. In addition, Campus Crusade for Christ offers "Character Clubs," a character-development curriculum that helps parents and teachers lead children to Christ and develop godly characteristics. For more information, see the list of Resources at the back of the book.

Children love to sing, so plan on having two or three songs. Christian bookstores carry a variety of gospel song visuals that you can purchase or you may wish to make your own as a family project.

Decide on the treats to serve. Keep decorations simple to avoid distractions and expense. If you are hosting a Birthday Party for Jesus, just use your holiday trimmings. For a daily or weekly meeting, you can make the snack the center of attention.

You may wonder, *When should I serve the snack?* You may offer something to eat either before the meeting starts or after it concludes. The advantage to eating first is that children are then more ready to settle down and hear the Bible story. Also, the snack will not disturb any counseling you may do after the story. But you may have a problem with latecomers who miss their treat. Serve the snack first if you have a prompt group or if your event will end near mealtime.

Waiting until after the meeting also has advantages. Children can take their treat home, and you don't have the problem of latecomers missing their snack. But you will have to reassure children who want to talk to you about spiritual matters that they will receive their snack in a few moments.

Be sure to *plan for children to participate*. Before the meeting begins and during snack time, ask them about their day; listen while they answer. The reason many children prefer attending a Bible club rather than watching television or a video is that they enjoy taking part in the activity. Often children will miss their favorite cartoons to hear a Bible story because they like the personal attention and interaction.

During the lesson time, use group involvement or a game to help them learn the memory verse; let them hold song visuals or use other ways to help them feel a part of the lesson. Compliment them freely with statements like, "You did such a good job holding that song," or, "I like the way you were so careful when you passed out the snack."

When it is time for the Bible lesson, ask the children to sit and pay attention. Try to create a mood that will not only help them hear what God has to say to them, but will also convey a respect for God's Word and for prayer.

Rehearse your Bible story until you can tell it by memory. You may want to practice telling the story to someone before the meeting. Keep your lesson short and to the point. Ten or fifteen minutes is long enough for children to sit still. Leave plenty of time after your lesson to invite children to receive Christ or to talk about spiritual matters.

Finally, *plan follow-up*. It's important to become a part of children's lives and to use your Bible club or party as a way to witness to their parents. Introducing yourself to the families will not only give you an opportunity to talk about Jesus, but it will help allay any fears the children's parents may have about what is going on at your event. You might say, "I just came over to meet you. I've had your child in our home and enjoyed him so much that I wanted to meet his parents." Your children's event then becomes a link to evangelizing your neighborhood.

The most effective follow-up, however, is getting the children to read the Bible for themselves, pray, and attend a church. You may want to purchase inexpensive Bibles for those who can read but do not have God's Word in their home. Try to involve your little guests in your church activities—without going against the wishes of their parents, of course. Your own children can also help get the other children excited about God's house. Sometimes a child's exuberant faith and your follow-up will persuade that child's parents to examine the claims of Jesus and begin attending church.

When everything has been planned, *pass out the invitations*. You may ask your own children to do this. Or you may do it as a way to meet your neighbors.

If your first event doesn't go smoothly, don't give up. Children don't expect perfection. If attendance is low, contact other children during the week and encourage them to attend the next meeting.

Common Questions About Children's Events

❧ **Where is the best place to hold a children's event?**
   Select a location that will cause the least distraction and in a room in your home where children can move around without breaking or harming anything. To minimize distractions, arrange seating with the children's backs to the windows, and place empty seats near the entrance so latecomers can join the

group without disturbing the meeting. You can also hold the event outside, but recognize that it may be more difficult to keep children's attention.

❧ What kind of snacks should I serve?

Children usually aren't particular about what they get and don't care for elaborate foods. If the food is messy, you may find yourself making many trips to the sink to wash little hands, or may have to clean fingerprints off your furniture. We recommend serving snacks that are healthy and not sticky. Pieces of fruit, small sugar-free cookies, or something else that is easy to eat will usually fit the occasion.

❧ What size group works well?

Any size group can be effective. You may be able to accommodate twenty to twenty-five children if your house is large enough, but limiting the size to ten or fifteen is preferable. A smaller group of five or six presents an excellent opportunity to get better acquainted with the children, lessens the possibility of discipline problems, and allows you to deal with each person on a spiritual basis. Even if you have only one child, you have an opportunity to share Christ's love.

❧ How can I handle discipline problems?

Many children don't know how to act in someone else's home. Setting simple guidelines early will let children know what to expect in your home and will eliminate many problems before they get started. Not only will your event go smoother, but your guests will learn to respect another person's home.

Emphasize that no one else should speak while you are talking during the Bible lesson. Keeping order will help the children consider God's Word precious. Refrain from saying, "Be quiet." Instead, when the group gets noisy, have the children raise their hands. When all hands are raised and the group is quiet, tell the children to lower their hands. This simple action helps the group discipline itself and helps the child learn to control himself.

❧ **What should I do if a parent objects to his child's involvement in my life-sharing event?**

Always respect the parent. You might say, "Would you like to visit one of our meetings? We sing songs, tell a Bible story, and serve a snack. We've enjoyed your son (or daughter) and would like to see him (her) continue to come. But we will respect your wishes."

If you suspect that a parent may object to his child attending, visit that home and extend a personal invitation. Remember, God is in control of your event, and He will work in the hearts of those who are open to His leading. It's not your responsibility to bring about the results.

Also, as you hold more events in your home, your neighbors may feel less uneasy. They may change their minds after their child continues to ask to come and after they talk to other parents who are enthusiastic about the parties. In addition, any new people who might move into the area may be less hesitant to send their children to an event that has become fairly well established.

❧ **How do I close the lesson and give an invitation to receive Christ?**

The person who teaches the lesson should give the invitation and help children who indicate that they have spiritual needs. When you close your lesson, ask them to bow their heads and close their eyes. You might say, "I'm the only one who will be looking. I want to ask you a very important question. Maybe there has been a time when you have asked Jesus to come into your life and be your Savior. Maybe it was at Sunday school or beside your bed with your mom or dad. If you prayed and asked Jesus to be your Savior and really meant it, then the Bible says He's in your life. He will never leave you. You can thank Him silently for that.

"But if you have never trusted Jesus to forgive your sins, and you know that you have sinned and would like to ask Jesus to come into your life as your Savior, let me know by raising your hand right now."

When you see one or more raised hands and sense that all the children have responded (don't press for decisions), say, "Okay, you can put your hand down now. I'm going to pray a little prayer." Then pray, "Thank You, Lord, for those who have just raised their hands to show that they want to ask You to come into their lives..."

When you finish praying, say, "Now, those of you who raised your hands, if you really meant it, come with me. For the rest of you, our hostess will give you a snack. For those who are coming with me, you will get your snack just a little bit later."

Take these children into another room or to a corner free from distractions. Sit on their level to talk to them personally, and give them each a booklet like the children's *Four Spiritual Laws* or the *Good News Comic Book*. Ask each person why he raised his hand to see if he understands the gospel message. Then go through the booklet until each child understands what it means to receive Christ as Savior.

Lead the children in a group prayer like the one in the booklet. To help them remember their decision to receive Christ as Savior, and to assure them that God answered their prayer, help them write their name on the decision page in the back of the booklet. Then record the date of their decision. Give them the booklet and tell them that it will help them remember that Jesus is in their life.

❧ **How can I be sure that the child responds to God's message of love and forgiveness and not to my urging?**

Put the condition before the response. For example, if you say, "I want you to raise your hand if..." that's what the child hears first and will respond before he understands the condition. But if you say, "If you realize that you have sinned and you believe that Jesus died for your sins and want Him to come into your life, then…," that's what the child hears first and will consider his decision before raising his hand.

Some children who already know Jesus as their Savior may respond simply because you are the only person they know who will talk to them on a spiritual level. Recognize that their spiritual needs are important and talk to them about their concerns.

Other children may not have another adult who will show them unconditional love and will respond for that reason. Reassure these children that their needs are important, too. Trying to meet every spiritual need these children bring to you is part of your ministry to them.

✿ How can I evaluate my teaching style?

One good method is to teach a practice lesson in front of several adult friends. Ask them to pretend that they are your young audience, then get their constructive feedback. If you have friends who are also holding children's events, meet with them and practice your lessons with each other. In addition, get feedback from your helper after the meeting.

The following is a summary of the steps in sequence to help you plan your event.

PLANNING THE EVENT	TIME
1. Begin praying.	Several weeks in advance
2. Find a helper.	
3. Select a date and location.	
4. Gather materials, make invitations.	A week in advance
5. Pass out invitations.	
6. Determine guidelines for children's behavior in your home.	

HOLDING THE EVENT	WHAT TO DO
1. Your guests arrive	Talk to the children, help them find seats, explain behavior guidelines for your event.
2. Song time	Invite the children to participate.
3. Bible lesson	Create a worshipful mood, gain children's attention.
4. Counseling	The teacher talks privately to children who need spiritual help.
5. Snack time	Invite the children to eat their snack in your home or take it with them. Remind them of your next meeting.
AFTER THE EVENT	WHAT TO DO
1. Evaluation	With your helper, discuss how you could teach the lesson more effectively, and decide on follow-up activities.
2. Follow-up	Pray for each child and his family. Visit families, build a relationship with children.
3. Begin planning for your next event	

Starting Small, Growing in Faith

If you feel too inexperienced to invite children into your home, think about how Jesus loved and cared for little ones. He spent time with them. He considered them just as important as adults. In fact, He used a child's faith as the example for our own.

Do not feel as if you must be experienced to minister to children. Before Bill and I had children, we decided with another couple who had a small child to prepare a Christmas dinner for youngsters who would not otherwise enjoy such a meal. We contacted a children's mission, and the directors gave us the names of several who would like to come.

We purchased gifts for each child and prepared a traditional Christmas dinner with turkey, dressing, and cranberry salad. The table was set with fine china and had a beautiful centerpiece.

Three boys and three girls came to our party. They were dressed in their Sunday best. In our inexperience, we let the children play games outdoors before the dinner. It had rained a day or two earlier, so they came inside with muddy shoes and soiled clothes.

When the children saw the elaborate meal, they asked, "Where are the chili beans and tortillas?" They were not excited about our idea of a favorite holiday feast.

But we had a delightful time. They opened their presents, and Bill told the Christmas story. They were so anxious to show their families what they had received and to tell them about the fun they had experienced that they were ready to go home earlier than we had planned.

After having our own children, we have become much wiser about entertaining children in our home. Now we have grandchildren, and love to tell them the gospel story and pray with them. Having worked and lived with these little ones, I am much more sensitive to their likes and needs, and have learned how to relate more effectively.

One summer when our granddaughter Rebecca was ten years old, she came to visit for a month. While she was here, I decided to host a tea party in her honor on July 1. We made it a mother-daughter, grandmother-granddaughter event with a patriotic theme that included red, white, and blue decorations. I asked a friend, Laura, who teaches sixth grade, to tell us what life was like for girls during the era when the Declaration of Independence was signed.

Laura did such a good job! She described our Christian heritage and how the Bible influenced the lifestyle of our nation when it was young. Then she passed out dainty gloves for each person to try on as she told about the needlework and dress worn by girls during those years. She also gave each guest a small circle of fabric and some potpourri from which we made fragrant sachets to take home.

I closed in prayer, then served dainty sandwiches and cookies that Rebecca had helped me make. We also served petit fours with red flowers on top, nuts, mints, chamomile tea, and coffee. What a memory the afternoon made for Rebecca and me!

This type of party can be adapted easily for a life-sharing event. You could invite a teen to speak or ask a woman who can share her faith in a manner that children understand to present the children's version of the *Four Spiritual Laws*.

Perhaps a party like this will spark your mind with other ideas for events. I encourage you to start where you are with the children in your area. As you grow in your entertaining skills, they will grow in their faith. And so will you!

Included in the Resources for Effective Life Sharing

❧ The Wordless Book: Lesson for Children

CHAPTER 15

Sponsoring a Teen Event

Vonette

T EENAGERS ARE always looking for excitement and fun. That's why my mother and dad sponsored so many parties in our home as the four of us children were growing up. The exciting times they hosted created memories that I still love to recall.

One of the best parties was my first teenage "partner" date. I was thirteen or fourteen, not old enough to date formally. I had a junior-high classmate named Major Caldwell whose mother invited several of his friends to their home for a dinner party. Each young man escorted a girl.

This was a spectacular evening for a young teen who was fascinated with the candlelight and the beautiful table setting. The place card was a whole walnut shell with a special note inside, tied together with a ribbon. Mrs. Caldwell served a delicious dinner, but I was impressed with the dessert. She made flaming puddings by placing a sugar cube soaked in lemon extract on each portion and igniting it with a match just before bringing it to the table. Her "flaming pudding" impressed me so much that it is now a tradition for our family Christmas dinner and for winter parties.

This social was a valuable investment of Mrs. Caldwell's time because of the enjoyment she gave us. The preparations must have caused her a lot of work, but the fun we had provided a lasting, happy memory for me.

Can you see how such an event could be used as an opportunity to share the true meaning of Christmas or the relevance of Christianity in a pull-apart world? I firmly believe parents have a great opportunity to reach teens for Christ by opening their homes to other young people. Let's look at ways we can plan, prepare, and host evangelistic events for teenagers.

Events for Teens

Through evangelistic entertaining, we not only have great opportunities to share Christ with unbelieving young people, but we also can help Christian teens learn how to introduce their friends to Jesus. Homes, schools, and neighborhoods can serve as bases for family ministry and as outreach places for church youth groups.

What you do for teenagers will provide lasting memories for them as they grow and mature in the Lord. Working with junior and senior high schoolers can be richly rewarding for you as well. You can help your own children get excited about seeing their friends come to know Jesus. And you can train Christian kids in how to share their faith in Christ. In the process, you will meet new students, and you will have a lot of fun!

Young people today don't have many opportunities to visit a godly home or even to meet Christian friends in a casual atmosphere. Your home can provide a safe place to talk about Jesus. These creative outreaches can be small or large, depending on the size of your home and the number of people you have available to help. But the activities should be simple and should meet the needs and interests of teens.

Your neighborhood and the nearest junior or senior high school will provide plenty of opportunities for hospitality. If you don't have teens living in your home and you choose your neighborhood as a point of outreach, you will need to build bridges.

Teen parties are not for amateurs. If you have never hosted events for junior or senior highers, invite other parents or youth leaders who have experience in working with this age group to help you.

Most teenagers don't receive enough positive attention from adults, and they look for someone with whom they can talk. Find out what their needs and interests are. One family made a baseball diamond in their cul-de-sac, and the neighborhood teens came to play baseball. Perhaps you know of several high school girls living near you. Offer to help them with their homework or give them tips on applying make-up. Use your expertise and their interests to build a friendship.

If you have teens in your home, you probably know many of their friends in the neighborhood. Sponsoring parties and other events in your home or neighborhood can even open doors of opportunity for reaching their school with the gospel.

You can also make home-based evangelistic entertaining a part of your youth activities at church. Youth leaders can set up a network of families who host parties and activities in their homes to reach a particular school or neighborhood around your church.

Developing Your Ministry to Teens

Teens can take a leadership role in planning, arranging, and hosting an event, and in the follow-up. Giving them the training and opportunity to have their "own" event and to counsel their peers will help them grow in their faith.

The kinds of events you could plan are numerous. But let us suggest one using the video series, *The Total Package*. This series has four episodes: (1) "Making Your Relationship Sure"; (2) "What Happens When I Mess Up?"; (3) "Holy Power"; and (4) "The Right Combination." You can obtain *The Total Package* by using the order information in the Resources. At the end of this chapter, we will offer alternative events you can sponsor. The steps for preparing, planning, arranging, conducting the event, and doing follow-up can be used with any of the suggestions we give in this chapter.

Preparing

In preparing for your evangelistic event, ask yourself: *What are the needs of the teens in my neighborhood? What are their interests?* Teens are attracted to people who care about them. Of course, they need Jesus as their Savior, but they probably aren't aware of that lack in their lives. Look for problems in areas such as companionship, self-control, or peer relationships. Most girls and boys at this age are trying to understand love, sex, and dating. They want to know how to get along with their friends and with adults. They may have family problems or difficulties in school.

Young people may be interested in sports teams, craft projects, or computers. They may be involved in clubs. You could interest them with tutoring or coaching sessions. And of course, they all get excited about food!

Invite people to help you with the event. Your own teens or other Christian young people can help plan and host the party. You will also need the assistance of other adults. We recommend a ratio of three adults for every five students, and no more than three non-Christian high schoolers for every teen who is a Christian. Too many unbelievers can discourage your ministering teens and can make an event difficult to manage.

The adults' role is to host and supervise. The Christian teens will be responsible for inviting their friends and ministering to them during the party. Explain to your young people that they will have to receive training on how to share their faith before they can attend the event. The purpose for this rule is twofold: to eliminate kids who just want to come for the fun and are not sincere about sharing their faith, and to help committed teens learn how to introduce others to Jesus. Plan several training sessions in which you view *The Total Package* video with the participating adults and teens and study the chapters in this book on how to present the *Four Spiritual Laws* and how to prepare and give your personal testimony.

The Total Package uses the booklet *Would You Like to Know God Personally?*, which is a more casual presentation of the *Four Spiritual Laws*. The methods used for presenting one booklet will work for the other. *Would You Like to Know God Personally?* is easily understood by this age group.

Begin praying for the group you want to reach for Christ. Involve the participating adults and teens in your praying. Together, ask for God's direction for the students who will attend the event and for God's power to present His message of love and forgiveness.

Choose your activity. Invite your teens to play a vital part in this decision. They know their peers and which activity would attract unbelieving junior or senior high students. Spontaneous gatherings can also be effective. Be open to visiting with teens at unscheduled times by encouraging your students to invite their friends to your home to hear a simple gospel presentation.

Planning

Involve your teens at the beginning stages of the planning. This will help them view the event as their own, rather than one that adults have planned for them. Make a planning chart for each person. We have included possible entries for hosting a video event in the following sample.

Question to ask	Materials and Schedules	Person Responsible	Time Involved
How will we pray for our event?	Weekly prayer groups in Sunday school classes or after school	Mr. Vinson for the adults Jeri for the teenagers	Begin praying now and continue through the follow-up time or beyond
What kind of activity or attraction will we have?	"Backward Compliment" ice-breaker game *The Total Package* video series, episode 1 Personal testimony	Jim Kelsey to introduce video Jason	Make decision several weeks in advance

Question to ask	Materials and Schedules	Person Responsible	Time Involved
What materials will we need?	*The Total Package*	Mr. Mason	
	Copies of magazines and Bibles that go along with the video		
	Copies of the *Know God Personally* booklets		
	Comment cards	Julie	
	Basket		
Who will we invite?	Juniors and seniors from Jackson High	Each Christian teen responsible to invite three friends	
What will happen during the activity?	Starting time	Everyone	7:00
	Ice-breaker game	Jim	7:05–7:25
	Introduce video	Kelsey	7:25–7:30
	View video		7:30–7:50
	Pass out cards and *Know God Personally* booklets	Brad and Jennifer	
	Personal testimony (refer to the booklets)	Jason	7:50–8:00
	One-to-one counseling/food	All teens	8:00–9:00
	Cleanup	Everyone	9:00–9:30
What invitations will we use?	Flyers to be given to the people we invite	Mrs. Aldrich to prepare	Give out one to two week in advance
What kind of food will we serve?	Pizza and soda	Mr. Aldrich	

Question to ask	Materials and Schedules	Person Responsible	Time Involved
When will we do our evaluation?	Paper, pencils	Everyone	Before the first follow-up session
What kind of follow-up will we do?	Comment cards, pencils, basket	Mrs. Mason to provide	Before each event, schedule place and time for follow-up
	One-to-one follow-up, which will lead to the three remaining video episodes	Christian teens to "divide and conquer"	After the event, review the comment cards and provide appropriate follow-up

This ice-breaker game works well with teens:

Backward Compliment

If you have more than ten young people, create groups of six to ten teens. Ask each group to form a circle on the floor. One teenager in each group starts the game by introducing the person on his left to the group. Then, to the person on his right, he whispers a compliment, in ten or fewer words, about the person he introduced. The person sitting on his right must whisper the compliment backward to the person sitting on her right. For example, if the compliment she hears is, "He has a nice smile," she would whisper, "Smile nice has he." The next person passes on the compliment correctly, and the following person says it backward, repeating the sequence until the compliment reaches the person who was just introduced. The last person in the circle repeats the compliment aloud to see how clear or distorted it has become. If the compliment is not understandable, the teenager who started the compliment will tell what he really said. Repeat the game until everyone has been introduced.

When planning, emphasize that the person responsible doesn't personally need to buy or do everything related to his assigned tasks, but that he must ensure it is all taken care of before the event. Here are some suggestions to make your planning more successful:

- Test the ice-breaker to see if it's successful with your students.

- Have enough workers with clear directions to handle all parts of the event.

- Be sure your television and videocassette player are in good working order.

- If you are having a speaker rather than a video, make sure your speaker and emcee understand when and how they are to participate.

- Provide a 3×5 card for comments, and decide how to collect the cards. (Placing a basket on the table for people to drop them into works well.)

- Decide where and when to have your subsequent sessions so the person who gives his testimony can encourage teens to attend the next three episodes of *The Total Package*.

- During your last training session, rehearse the event. First, play the ice-breaker game, then ask someone to introduce the video. After the video, ask teens to pass out the comment cards and *Would You Like to Know God Personally?* booklets. Have a student share his testimony and introduce the booklet.

- The speaker will point out the prayer in the booklet and invite teens to pray silently with him. Ask Christian teens to "divide and conquer" during the refreshment time to talk to non-Christians one-on-one to find out what they thought of the video. The Christian teens should use the *Would You Like to Know God Personally?* booklet to ask these questions: *Have you ever made this kind of commitment before? Would you like to right now?*

Keep your party as simple as possible. Just having Christian students invite friends to hear a gospel presentation can be quite effective. Use the refreshment time to build bridges to the teens and ask them about their spiritual lives.

Setting Rules

Just like younger children, teenagers sometimes behave improperly. Before the party, set rules with your ministering teens and participating adults so that you can help to avoid problems. The rules should teach respect for the home you are using and for the seriousness of the video message. Here is a basic list of rules to which you can add your own:

- All rooms other than the one you are using are off-limits.
- Discourage teens from using the stereo or any Walkmans they have brought.
- Christian students are to arrange to pick up their friends and take them home.
- Determine a signal that lets everyone know when the noise level is too high.
- Pay attention during the video session.
- Handle the food properly. (No food fights, etc.)

Make sure everyone helping with the event understands the rules and emphasize that each person is responsible for enforcing them during the event.

Follow-Up

Follow-up involves three steps. First, *talk to each non-Christian teen to learn if he prayed the prayer at the end of the video* or made a decision after the personal testimony. Christian teens should use the "divide and conquer" method to accomplish this. During the refreshment time, instruct them to talk to each guest individually to determine his spiritual needs or help the teen with any commitment he wants to make. Use the *Would You Like to Know God Personally?* booklets for this step.

Second, *encourage guests to attend Bible studies* that will help them grow in their faith. Soon after the event, review the comment cards and call the people who indicated they made a decision for

Christ. Invite them to the subsequent sessions. Usually, teens should contact the guests they brought to the party.

Third, *evaluate your event to see how you can be more effective at your next party.* Carefully review the comments on the cards during your evaluation for the teens' response to the party. Also, discuss with the Christian teens how the party went.

Campus Crusade's Student Venture ministry can help you reach out to teens. Ask the staff about the Student Venture group nearest you. Student Venture also has a ministry called VITAL LINC to help coach people who don't live in areas near a Student Venture staff member. They will help equip you to develop a ministry to a high school in your city. For further information or materials, see the Resources.

Coke-In

Several years ago, Mr. and Mrs. McGoldrick and their eighth-grade daughter, Debbie, attended a LIFE seminar in Grand Rapids, Michigan. As a result of the training, they began sharing their faith in their neighborhood and at work. Debbie got excited about introducing her friends to the Lord. One day in the school lunch-room, she read through the *Four Spiritual Laws* with her close friend who received Christ as her Savior. Soon, several other friends came to know Christ and they began a small Bible study. Debbie's parents helped by leading a "basic training" for high school students in their basement. The McGoldricks taught the Christian teens how to share their faith in local parks, on beaches, and at area high school hangouts.

The Christian teens asked God to show them how they could reach more teens for Christ. One evening, they planned a party they called a "Coke-In." They began with one party, and the idea spread. Before long, there were parties at four or five locations on the same evening. The hosts and hostesses met before the parties to pray together. Afterward, the phone lines would buzz as the Christian students called each other to see what God had done.

These young people shared their idea with local churches and youth groups. Debbie and her friends even presented the format during a Campus Crusade for Christ college-age conference in Chicago. The events changed Debbie's perspective on life. She learned how exciting a life of serving God could be. After graduating from high school, Debbie attended a Bible college then joined our Student Venture staff, where she still serves.

A Coke-In party uses the life-sharing format with these differences. Each Christian teen invited to the party must bring at least one non-Christian friend. Prepare two sets of invitations, one for the Christians who will attend and the other for the friends they will invite. Here are samples you can adapt for your Coke-In.

You Are Invited to a Coke-In!

Where:

When:

Time:

Come *only* if you are bringing a friend you would like to introduce to Christ in a personal way!

You Are Invited to a Coke-In!

Where:

When:

Time:

Directions to the home:

The refreshments include Coke as a beverage, of course, and games such as Twister, ping pong, pool, horseshoes, jarts, badminton, or other group games. After the game time, the host or hostess passes out *Four Spiritual Laws* booklets to each person and introduces a Christian friend who presents the *Four Spiritual Laws* by reading through the booklet while guests follow along. When each person has had a chance to silently pray the prayer, the host distributes comment cards for the teens to fill out.

If you host a Coke-In, follow the life-sharing plan for follow-up as given in Chapter 9 to help new Christians become involved in small group Bible studies and to encourage other believers to grow in their faith.

Other Kinds of Events

There is virtually no limit to the kinds of evangelistic parties you can have with teens. We'd like to suggest a few to stimulate your thinking.

Valentine Outreach

For this couples' event, advertise a topic such as "What Is True Love, Anyway?" For an ice-breaker, play "The Dating Game." Couples answer questions to see who knows the most about their partner. After the game, have someone give a talk on the different kinds of love: the "if" love, the "because" love, and the "anyhow" love. Then ask a Christian teen to give a personal testimony on how much God's love has done for him or her.

Super Bowl Blast

Invite teens to your home to watch the Super Bowl and eat snacks. At half-time, ask a Christian teen to tell how God plays fair and how He sent His Son to pay for all of our sins (penalties). This will also work for Monday Night Football.

Brain Bash

Invite students who have a 3.5 GPA or higher for an evening of studying, games, and pizza. Plan a discussion time on creation versus evolution or another academic/religious topic. Invite a Christian student to give a personal testimony on knowing God as Creator and Savior.

Slumber Party

Invite Christian girls and their non-Christian friends for overnight fun. Play games, make homemade candy, or ask a beautician to give beauty tips. Discuss how God creates inner beauty by giving us new life.

Backyard Volleyball

You will need a large backyard for this. Plan a barbecue, play volleyball, then set aside a time for personal testimonies and discussion about how we can win in the game of life.

10-Foot Banana Split

This is great fun for an outside, summer party. Set up tables in a long row, and let the teens make and eat their 10-foot banana split. Build a long V-shaped trench from boards and wrap it with aluminum foil. Fill the trench with bananas, ice cream, and all the fixings. Wrap up the party with a speaker or video. Your topic could be "Knowing God Is Better Than Eating a Colossal Banana Split!"

Popcorn Party

How many ways can you flavor popcorn? Ask each person to bring a topping, then pop corn and let the teens flavor it any way they like. Some suggestions are onion or garlic powder, herbed butter, dry pudding, peanuts, caramel, and fudge. Have the kids watch an evangelistic video while they eat their popcorn.

"Right From Wrong" Pizza Party

The Josh McDowell Ministry recently released a new book to teach students the importance of knowing and choosing right from wrong. Most junior and senior high young people are grappling with moral decisions and want to know more about how to conduct themselves. Bringing up topics like sexual purity, honesty, and integrity will lead to evangelistic opportunities. Call the Josh McDowell Ministry at (214) 907-1000 to get more information on the book and other available resources.

Along with hosting teen events, follow God's leading in building bridges to their families. Dale and Mary Eggelston learned how hospitality can influence a family.

The Eggelstons enjoy hiking trips with their teenage children. They invited a family of nonbelievers to join them for a weekend camping trip. During the weekend, the Eggelstons continued their custom of thanking God for the food at meal times and gathering to pray and read the Bible in the morning and evening. They asked their friends to join them.

After the second morning of devotions, the Eggelstons heard the wife say to her husband, "Perhaps we would have less conflict in our home if we had devotions and prayer together every day."

The family that is not exposed to vital Christianity has little idea of how biblical principles work in daily life. But this couple had watched the Eggelstons relate with each other, deal with teen–parent differences, and handle crisis situations.

The greatest sermon preached is a life lived before others. This principle applies just as effectively in working with teens. The Christian home is one of the greatest witnessing tools in reaching out to young people and their parents.

CHAPTER 16

Enjoying Christmas Celebrations

Barbara

HAVE YOU ever said this? "I'd like to share my faith with my neighbors, but it seems so hard to find a time when they will *really* listen."

Christmas is one season when most of your friends and neighbors think of Jesus—at least superficially. It is a season when homes, stores, even city streets take on a religious spirit.

At the same time, people feel empty and lonely during the holidays. The greatest number of suicides occur during this season because of disappointments and unmet expectations.

Tragically, most people overextend their calendars and pocketbooks and have little understanding of how significant Christmas is or how meaningful it can be. Instead, they shop, bake goodies, and plan parties without acknowledging the beauty and significance of Christ's birth. Adults battle holiday crowds at the mall to fulfill children's long wish lists, and festivities do not turn into the uplifting, glorious events that people expect or that they remember from their childhood.

But the season still holds enough Christian tradition and sentiment that you and I can take advantage of the spirit to present the gospel in a nonthreatening, relevant way. That's why Christmas celebrations are so effective. Joyce Bademan, founder and national director of a ministry called Christmas Gatherings, says, "Christmas is a wonderful season to make Christ's message real and meaningful. People's hearts are unusually open and receptive to spiritual thoughts and to being together. They feel honored to be invited to a party where there will be people they know or would like to know."

Imagine yourself attending a celebration at a festively decorated home, enjoying holiday food, and sharing your favorite Christmas traditions and memories with friends and neighbors. While your mind is focused on the joy of the season, a speaker gives a short talk on the real meaning of Christmas. When the gospel is presented, your heart is open and willing to receive the One for whom the celebration is given. As you pray to ask Jesus to be your Savior, you receive priceless holiday gifts to take home: true peace, eternal life, and overflowing joy.

Helping others receive God's gift of His Son is what makes Christmas celebrations so exciting. Many men and women have discovered the joy of hosting these events. Here are two examples:

Linda Patterson

"I had a Christmas gathering last night and was so overjoyed and thankful to God. He has allowed me to share the good news with twenty-five to thirty women this Christmas season. We planted many seeds and even saw several people accept Christ."

Mary Lehman

"This past Christmas, a neighbor decided to open her home for a Christmas gathering. She and another hostess invited me to be the speaker. As I shared the gospel, I indicated that we would like to start a neighborhood Bible study if anyone would be interested. I asked the guests to give their response on comment cards. Later, the three of us wept and rejoiced before the Lord when twelve out of seventeen women indicated an interest in studying God's Word together. We have been meeting for twelve weeks, and these neighbors have invited others."

Joyce Bademan tells how the idea of Christmas Gatherings has spread. When Pam Adler and a few friends heard about this method of sharing their faith, they hosted a coffee that lead to a Bible study. The coffees and Bible studies multiplied. This past year, three busloads of neighbors who had attended life-sharing Christmas celebrations were taken by their hostesses to attend a Billy Graham Crusade.

Jeanne Frasch began hosting events through her church and organized Bible studies with interested women. Currently, two hundred women attend these studies.

Dave Gibson, pastor of Grace Church in Edina, Minnesota, became so excited about Christmas Gatherings that he began speaking at couples' events. Now he and his wife also host parties.

These examples show the effectiveness and fun of hosting life-sharing events during the holiday season. But will people take time out of their busy schedules to attend a party like this? Definitely, yes!

During the Christmas season, people are searching for togetherness and meaning. Most television shows, movies, and books portray the holidays as a time when friends gather and families celebrate together and everyone buys perfect gifts for friends and relatives. In reality, many people are isolated and too busy, and they have a difficult time scheduling an hour or two for a relaxed visit with anyone. They would love to be invited to a party where they are loved and appreciated, and where they can relax and think about the season. Let me share an example of someone who experienced this response.

Celebrating the Joy

Many years ago, Joyce Yancey of Birmingham, Alabama, began a home-based ministry of small group Bible studies with teens and college-age singles. Soon older women began attending also, and the studies multiplied in number. Then the Lord began to impress the women to reach out to their families with the gospel. As a result, each December group members began hosting a simple covered-dish Christmas dinner called Celebration. The event began to attract so many people that Celebration grew to a "dutch treat" meal in a moderately priced restaurant. Bible class members donated favorite goodies, candles, ribbons, and greenery, and brought their families and friends to the event.

Attendance kept rising until the group outgrew the restaurants. As the leaders prayed about the problem, the Lord provided a beautiful country club facility. This past year, more than five hundred guests attended the Celebration, and 16 percent of them indicated that they had received Christ!

"We hand-craft everything we can for the event," Joyce explains. Bible class members send out handmade invitations to their friends and families. Some families help plan and organize the event. Members of a men's group called the "Carpenter's Men," which grew out of the Celebration ministry, craft wooden centerpieces for each table and a gift for each guest. Fathers and sons—some of whom have been introduced to the Lord through the dinners—work side-by-side.

The core committee and many other volunteers make name tags, place cards, and invitations, and decorate scrolls for each plate. They plan table settings, lighting details, the sound system, and seating arrangements.

On the day of the Celebration, chairmen, core groups, and committee members meet for prayer, then swing into action. Every guest is individually greeted and seated. The program features music specials and Santa and his elf who give handmade gifts to every guest. A speaker presents the true reason for celebration—Jesus Christ. As in any life-sharing event, guests record their decisions and responses on comment cards. Not only do they respond with enthusiastic praise for the fun and fellowship, but those involved in the ministry are just as thrilled.

People come from the surrounding cities to attend Celebration—even as far away as Huntsville, Alabama, and Atlanta, Georgia. Many of those who volunteer their time were introduced to Jesus through this ministry.

Whether your Christmas celebration is a one-time, casual event or develops into an annual tradition, you will experience the love and joy that the true meaning of Christmas brings to your neighbors. We encourage you to involve your family—from Grandma and Grandpa to the little ones—or your church ministry circle in a life-sharing celebration at Christmas.

Planning Your Christmas Celebrations

Christmas parties follow the same basic format as other life-sharing events. If you feel God leading you to open your home during the holidays, review Chapters 6 through 11 to remind yourself how to plan, set up, and host an event.

Decide the kind of Christmas celebration you will schedule. Make it as formal or casual as you feel comfortable with, and one that your friends will enjoy. A light evening dessert with beverage works well with busy schedules, and it's easy to plan the refreshments around your holiday baking. Other ideas include a Christmas candlelight dinner, brunch, noon luncheon, or a morning or afternoon coffee. You can bring out your most elegant dinnerware or use festive paper products. Either approach works well.

I enjoy decorating every nook and cranny of our home and begin right after Thanksgiving. I ask the Lord to show me what to do and thank Him for the creative ideas He gives me. We encourage you to follow your holiday schedule and traditions when you plan a life-sharing party. Make your event fit your lifestyle.

Select a date within the first two weeks in December. Parties held later tend to conflict with other seasonal activities. Then invite your guests. Handwritten invitations are a nice touch, or adapt the sample Christmas invitations in this chapter. Because mailboxes get heaped with cards and letters around the holidays and your invitation may get lost at the bottom of the pile, we suggest that, wherever practical, you hand-deliver your invitations. For more information on how to invite guests and plan a party, review Chapters 6 and 7.

Ask someone to speak during your party. Instruct him or her to prepare a 15- to 30-minute talk with a Christmas theme and a clear gospel presentation. You may want to reproduce these hand-outs for your speaker:

- ❧ Personal Testimony Preparation Guidelines
- ❧ Personal Testimony Worksheet
- ❧ Personal Testimony Evaluation
- ❧ Speaker's Worksheet
- ❧ How to Present the *Four Spiritual Laws*

Another option is for your speaker to give the sample talk included on the following pages, which is taken from Joyce Bade-man's *Christmas Gatherings Resource Manual.* Joyce suggests asking guests to share their Christmas traditions, then inviting your speaker to give a 10- to 15-minute talk on a Christmas theme into which the gospel message is woven.

Whichever option you choose, pray with your speaker. Suggest topics such as the following:

- ❧ Jesus, God's Greatest Gift
- ❧ The Real Meaning Behind Christmas Traditions
- ❧ Why Christmas Means So Much to Me

For more help on preparing and giving a talk, see Chapters 10 and 11.

Here is one of the talks Joyce suggests, which your speaker can adapt easily for your party.

Christmas Gathering Sample Talk

I have enjoyed hearing about your favorite Christmas memories and traditions. So many of them involve giving and receiving of gifts. I'd like you to consider for a moment: What would be the greatest gift one person could give another?

If you have served in the military, you might say that the greatest gift would be to lay down your life so that your comrade might live. For some, it might be a winning sweepstakes ticket or a dream car. For others, it may be finding a steady job, having good health, or enjoying meaningful relationships with family members.

For the next few minutes, I'd like to share with you what I consider to be the greatest gift ever given.

"God so loved the world (that's you and me), that He gave His only Son, that whoever believes in Him would not perish but would have eternal life." These words are from the Bible.

Two thousand years ago, on that first Christmas night, God came to this earth in the person of the baby Jesus. In fact, one of the names given to the baby (at God's command) was Emmanuel, which literally means "God is with us."

Do you know why God did this? Because He loves us! God loves us so personally that He calls us by name. He loves us just the way we are, with all our failures, faults, and bad habits.

Fortunately for us, Jesus didn't remain a baby, but grew to be a man. He was a carpenter by trade, a working man just like you and me. He lived on this earth as fully man and, at the same time, fully God.

In His early 30s, Jesus paid the penalty for all the nasty, selfish things that you and I have ever thought, said, or done. Jesus took my punishment and yours by willingly dying on the cross for us. He was buried, but on the third day He rose again. He lives today.

You see, God is a holy God. He is perfect and flawless. Man, on the other hand, is imperfect, marred by sin. Do you know what sin is? It is anything that separates you from God. You might be saying to yourself, "Well, I'm a good person. I go to church. I'm not a sinner." But think just for a moment about some of the selfish things you've done: those angry outbursts, those unkind thoughts. Those are sins, and they separate us from God.

The Bible also says that forgiveness of sin is not earned. It is a gift of God, so we can't brag about it. God does not expect nor want us to earn our forgiveness by pulling ourselves up by our own boot straps. We will never be good enough. He wants us to simply accept and receive forgiveness and eternal life as His free gift through faith in Jesus Christ. Everyone must make his or her own decision about receiving this gift.

I once heard a lawyer tell a true story about a legal case in Georgia. I want to share it with you, because I think it's a great analogy of what I've been talking about.

A man named Wilson, a convicted felon, was scheduled to die in the Georgian penal system. Due to certain irregularities in his trial, the Governor—and later the President of the United States—granted Wilson a pardon. The problem was that Wilson, apparently frustrated and embittered about his situation, refused the pardon. The authorities faced a dilemma. The prosecution said, "Execute him!" The defense said, "Let him go free." They appealed the case to the United States Supreme Court.

In writing for the Supreme Court, Justice Marshall acknowledged the dilemma. There was a pardon, and Wilson's name was on it. It was a valid pardon from the President of the United States. The problem was that the defendant was still guilty. He was found guilty by a jury. Understand that a pardon does not remove the guilt—it just covers it. A pardon does not make a guilty person innocent. Wilson was still guilty.

Justice Marshall said that a pardon is a gift, an act of grace, which is basically undeserved favor. As a gift, it is given, but it must also be received. A person can choose to receive the pardon or not. Wilson chose to reject the pardon. Therefore, his guilt was not covered, and since he was still guilty, he had to pay the penalty for his crimes. In carrying out the dictates of the Supreme Court decision, the State of Georgia executed Wilson.

Today all of us are in a similar dilemma. We are guilty because of sin in our lives, but a pardon is available that will cover our guilt. We have a choice. We can receive Jesus Christ by inviting Him into our lives and thus receive forgiveness and eternal life. Or we can choose to reject Him, or avoid making a decision at all, which is the same as rejecting Him.

Jesus said, "I am the way, the truth, and the life. No one comes to the Father except by Me." He also says, "Behold, I stand at the door and knock. If anyone hears My voice and invites Me in, I will come in and eat with him and live with him forever."

God has given us free choice. We can choose to keep Jesus out of our lives, or we can choose to invite Him in. Several years ago, unlike Wilson who chose to refuse his pardon, I chose to accept mine from God. I didn't deserve it then, and I don't deserve it now. But I received it all the same.

You will have to make your own decision. In closing, I'd like to give you an opportunity to receive your pardon by praying a prayer similar to the one I prayed. Pray silently along with me.

Dear Heavenly Father, I know that I've done many selfish, self-centered things, and I confess them to You. I believe that Jesus Christ died for me and for my sins, and I want to receive my pardon. I invite Him to come into my life and take control. Thank You, Father, for not giving up on me and for loving me. It is in Jesus' name that I pray. Amen.

If you prayed with me and sincerely meant it, God heard your prayer and that Jesus Christ has come into your life.

I want to thank you for giving me an opportunity to share the most important gift ever given. Would you do me a favor right now by writing your impressions about this evening on one of these cards. Did you like having the chance to get together? Did you like the food? How did you like what I shared tonight? Good, bad, or indifferent, I'd like to have your comments.

If you prayed along with me tonight, place an "X" on your card. (Host or hostess' name) would like to get together with you for four weeks in January for a short Bible study. If you are interested, indicate that on your card along with your name and phone number. (At this point, turn the program over to the host.)[1]

Hosting Your Christmas Celebration

After serving refreshments, you may choose to begin with a sharing time to put your guests at ease and to help them focus on the Christmas season. You might say something like the following:

One of the things I find enjoyable about the holiday season is learning about other Christmas traditions. Why don't we take a few moments to share some of our holiday traditions? Perhaps you make festive foods, celebrate unique

---

[1] Adapted from *Christmas Gatherings Resource Manual*, by Joyce Bademan, director of Christmas Gatherings, a ministry to help train others for evangelistic entertaining during the Christmas season.

customs, or have special family plans this year. To give you a chance to think of what you might say, I'll go first.

Allow your guests to speak as they feel led. After about twenty minutes, say, "It's been so much fun to hear about your traditions. It seems like we've just started. Maybe we can share more of them later." Then introduce your speaker who will give the talk, present the gospel, and instruct guests to fill out comment cards as suggested in Chapter 11.

After the speaker concludes, offer your guests more refreshments. While people talk, be available for anyone who desires more information about an upcoming Bible study or who wants to ask spiritual questions. As soon as your guests leave, meet with your helpers to glance through the comment cards, and plan for follow-up. Chapter 9 will help you get started.

I would like to share several examples of life-sharing events that I have held during the holiday season.

Christmas Tea

This year, Howard and I will host a tea for both men and women. Instead of inviting a speaker, we will select a reading. Two of our favorites are *A Cup of Christmas Tea* by Tom Hegg and *The Angel's Point of View* by J. B. Phillips. Both are sold in gift shops.

A Cup of Christmas Tea is a story with a caring, loving family message. When we used it in past years, we have seen tears in many eyes. Since the gospel is not clearly presented, we also share the *Four Spiritual Laws*.

The Angel's Point of View is a story of an older, wiser angel showing a young companion the splendors of God's universe and the glory of Christ's visit to planet earth. We enjoy this story so much that we share it with our family and friends every Christmas.

Christmas Neighborhood Celebration

This Christmas, Howard and I will also host an appetizer buffet. This event works well in a neighborhood where the people know each other. On the invitations, we request that each couple bring an appetizer to serve twenty-four people. The hostess usually provides the dessert. You can simplify this event by serving your own appetizers.

Before the event, we ask children in our neighborhood if they will perform the Christmas story for us. Their parents help them with the script and costumes. Between the buffet and dessert, the children act out the story. Then Howard closes with brief remarks on the subject, "God's Gift to Everyone." When he finishes, we serve dessert and have fun!

Here is what we put on the invitations. Adapt this format to create your own.

Ringing in Our Second Annual Christmas Celebration

At the home of Howard and Barbara Ball
1123 Oak Road
5:00 p.m., Saturday, December 7

Come for an appetizer buffet and a chance to meet old and new neighbors, as well as see children present a play called "The Very First Christmas." The play will be followed by brief remarks from Howard Ball. We are excited about this celebration and look forward to seeing you.

R.S.V.P. 446-7667

Please bring an appetizer to serve 24.

Christmas Friends Caroling Celebration

When we lived in California, we invited new acquaintances and old friends to a caroling party. This event became a yearly tradition for our neighbors.

One year, we asked Bob Henley, a man very active in the community and a wonderful song leader, to serve as song director. In the invitation, we encouraged our guests to wear hats and scarves to dramatize cold, snowy weather in our balmy California climate. We obtained music sheets in large print so our group could read the songs by flashlight.

As soon as everyone arrived, we passed out small bells to ring during the songs. Then we went caroling in our neighborhood. When finished, we returned to our home for dessert.

While our guests enjoyed their food, we presented our short program. Some years, we asked a couple to give a testimony. During other parties, Howard briefly shared the Christmas story and one time a friend brought her guitar and sang for us.

This is the invitation we used for the caroling party:

Here We Go-A-Caroling

When: Saturday, December 7

Time: 5:30 p.m.

Where: The home of Howard and Barbara Ball
1123 Oak Road

Please bring an appetizer to serve 24. Dress for caroling by wearing winter hats and scarves. We will supply the music and bells!

Adapt this to your neighborhood and situation. You could host a sing-a-long to recorded Christmas carols or join a larger caroling group, such as a charity organization, then meet back at your home for dessert.

If you are interested in encouraging a Christmas ministry in your church or area and would like more resources and training, see the Resources to order the *Christmas Gatherings* manual. May the Lord bless you as you make His birth real in the lives of your friends, co-workers, neighbors, and loved ones.

CHAPTER 17

Hosting a Video Presentation

Vonette

ONE OF THE most effective ways to introduce others to Jesus and to help believers grow and mature in their Christian faith is through hosting a video presentation in your home. This has been very successful in many parts of the world.

Dr. Jack Hayford, pastor of the well-known Church on the Way in Van Nuys, California, asked his congregation to use the *"JESUS"* film in video format for home-based evangelism. The *"JESUS"* film is a dramatic re-creation of the life, ministry, death, and resurrection of our Lord that has been shown all over the world. This film has been translated into more than 320 languages and has been used to bring millions to our Savior. Four hundred members from the church agreed to show the video in their homes on a designated evening before Easter. As a result, more than four hundred people came to know Christ that night. That was more than double the church's best Easter evangelism outreach to date!

In today's technologically advanced society, a video captures an audience who may not be open to other methods of evangelism. A video is easy to prepare and to present. Here are some remarks from several people who have used a video presentation in their home:

"For years, my husband and I have been really concerned about our neighbors, and we wanted to be witnesses. I don't see myself as an evangelist or a door-to-door person, but this gave me a neutral ground on which to reach somebody, and the outcome of it has really increased my faith."

"This [video presentation] made it easy for me to witness about Jesus Christ because by showing the video at my house, I didn't have to do any work except to invite the people."

"Basically, this is one of the first times I have witnessed, and it broke the ice."

One young couple were concerned about people they knew who were not acquainted with Jesus, but they had no idea how to begin a witness. They decided a video presentation would work for them, so they invited friends from work and from their neighborhood. Fifteen people came that night. Through the video, the couple were able to share Christ's love and forgiveness with their guests and to see new opportunities to witness to some of those who didn't attend. As a result, a Bible study was formed with five people.

Another woman was new in her neighborhood but wanted to be a witness. She invited a large number of people, including her husband's business associates, to her event. Since she didn't know many of her prospective guests, she had no idea who would come. Thirty-five people came, and she was able to form a Bible study group with persons who responded.

A Unique Presentation

Perhaps you have friends who have never heard a clear presentation of the gospel. Yet they wouldn't feel comfortable joining a group of people in your home to hear a speaker. Or you have a heavy work schedule and don't have time to prepare an elaborate party or meal. Then a video presentation may work well for you. Whether inviting business associates, family groups, singles, or relatives, the principles are basically the same as for any type of life-sharing event.

What are the advantages of hosting a video presentation?

First, *the video gives a credible and complete explanation of the gospel message.* Although preparing your personal testimony is still an important element in relating your faith at a meeting such as this, the video will help you introduce others to Jesus Christ in a thorough, interesting way.

Second, *a video is a nonthreatening medium for most people.* The dramatic action in the film lets them see and hear the story of Jesus.

Third, *nonbelievers may be more relaxed in your home watching a video than they would be in a church building.* They can concentrate on the story without many distractions.

Fourth, *the video presents a timely, challenging invitation to receive Christ at its conclusion.* That helps you or your co-host lead the discussion afterward into spiritual matters.

You can select any video that concludes with an invitation to receive Christ. Barbara and I recommend the *"JESUS" Home Video Package*, a complete, step-by-step package that contains a training film hosted by Pat Boone, the 82-minute version of the *"JESUS"* video, a facilitator's guide, a host resource manual that includes a five-week follow-up Bible study guide, comment cards, and *Who Is This Jesus?*, an informative magazine for those who attend your video showing. The package also contains excellent suggestions on how to conduct your event and some easy-to-use Bible study lessons for follow-up sessions. Another excellent follow-up tool is the *Knowing Jesus Personally* video and magazine, produced by Campus Crusade for Christ, Canada. See the Resources for ordering information.

Another effective video is *A Man Without Equal.* This thirty-minute program explores the unique birth, earthly life, teachings, death, and resurrection of our Lord. The breathtaking portraits from the great masters and the inspiring re-creations of Jesus' life will grip your guests. The *Man Without Equal* video is a very effective way to present life sharing. You can obtain each of these resources from your local Christian bookstore or use the order form at the back of this book. Adapt the following instructions for the video you choose.

Using the Home Video Strategy

If you have carefully read and studied the first nine chapters in this book, you will have a good foundation for hosting a video presentation. Turn to the Resources and use the "Planning Schedule," "Hostess Checklist," and "How to Present the *Four Spiritual Laws*" to plan and prepare for your event.

If you are inviting a large group of people who are not close friends, ask someone to co-host your video showing. This person plays a critical role by being responsible for the spiritual aspects of your presentation. This will allow you to concentrate on greeting your guests and serving refreshments. Ask your co-host to introduce the video and close the presentation after the showing is over. He or she will instruct your guests how to fill out the comment cards and then collect them. Both you and your co-host should be familiar with how to present the *Four Spiritual Laws* or another simple and clear gospel presentation.

You will need the following materials:

* A television and a VCR
* *A Man Without Equal* or *"JESUS"* video
* 3×5 cards (for comment cards)
* Pens or pencils
* A *Four Spiritual Laws* booklet for each person attending

On the day of the video showing, arrange the meeting room so everyone will have a good view of the television screen and not be distracted by latecomers or by glare from windows. Ask the co-host to put the materials for discussion on the most centrally located table or chair.

Greet your guests warmly as they arrive. When it is time to begin the meeting, ask your guests to find a seat. Introduce your co-host who then will give the reason for the showing and explain that he or she will be handing out cards for each guest to record comments following the video.

Here is an example of what your co-host could say:

Before we see the video, I want to thank Brian for providing his home and the refreshments. Both he and I are excited about what Jesus has been doing in our lives. That is why we have asked all of you to see this video. It shows who Jesus is and how He has changed the course of history.

After we have seen the video, we'll have a short discussion time. Then, I would like each of you to comment on the video and this evening's discussion. When we finish, we'll have something to eat and spend time getting to know each other.

I'm going to start the video now. I believe you will find it challenging.

Dim the lights and start the video. At the conclusion, give a copy of the *Four Spiritual Laws* to each person and go through the booklet together. The *Man Without Equal* video includes thought-provoking questions for discussion, which you may also use.

Next, ask your co-host to do the following:

* Pass out the 3×5 cards and pencils. Ask the viewers to write their names, addresses, and telephone numbers on one side of the card.

* On the other side, ask them to write the following:

    1. Brief answers to these questions:

       Have you received Jesus as your Savior and Lord? When?

       Are you interested in learning more about how Jesus can change your life?

    2. Specific comments about the video and the discussion

When your co-host finishes, describe the small-group Bible study you will be starting. Explain that you will contact each person later about the time and place for your first meeting. If some in your group are Christians who are growing in their relationship to Christ, challenge them to join your Bible study for fellowship and spiritual growth. If some guests are not believers or have just made a decision to follow Christ, encourage them to attend the Bible study to learn more about the most amazing person in history, Jesus Christ.

Thank your guests for coming and explain that you will be available for any questions during the refreshment time. Then dismiss your group with a prayer similar to this one:

> Dear Lord Jesus, thank You for Your presence here in this place. Thank You for each person you brought here. May the truth of Jesus penetrate each of our lives to make us the person you want us to be. In His name. Amen.

Collect the cards and serve the refreshments. While others are chatting and eating, make sure you and your co-host are available to talk with anyone who may want to receive Christ as Savior or who has questions. If someone is unsure of how to receive Christ, go through the *Four Spiritual Laws* booklet with that person.

After your guests leave, look over the 3×5 cards and plan when you can contact each person. To do so, send a follow-up letter and make a follow-up appointment. For more help, see the "Sample Follow-Up Letter" and "Scheduling and Conducting a Follow-up Appointment" in the Resources.

Through your obedience and the power of the Holy Spirit, you can change your world for Christ with a video presentation and effective follow-up. In the process, you will gain lifelong friendships and influence the lives of many people. And you will experience the joy of hospitality and the excitement that Christ gives to those who earnestly desire to serve others in His name.

CHAPTER 18

You Can Make a Difference

Vonette

BILL'S MOTHER, Mary Lee, was an inspiration to me. A well-educated woman, she enjoyed classical literature and cherished her Bible. She married a cattle rancher and gave birth to eight children. Although life on the ranch was not easy in rural America at that time, she lived a vital Christian witness before her family and friends. Mother Bright made her home a haven for the family, and cared for neighbors in need. Her home was so popular that she often did not know how many places to set for a meal. Whenever anyone in the community mentioned the most godly person they knew, Mrs. Bright's name always came up first. Because of her faithful example and hospitality, her influence is still felt around the world through her children and friends.

Of course, life today is much different from what Mother Bright faced. But the principles for which she worked and lived remain. A godly home can have a profound influence on our hectic, self-centered society. The family or single person who opens the door to others stands out against the backdrop of a lonely, uncaring world.

Many factions in our culture fight desperately to topple the values by which our society has lived. The Christian heritage we have taken for granted for so long has broken down, and many people no longer discern right from wrong according to biblical principles. The evening news shows us conflict everywhere—in the furor over school policies; in local, state, and national legislative disputes; in fights for community standards. You may have noticed the impact of the disintegrating moral fiber in your own neighborhood: couples contemplating divorce; children caught in the middle of custody fights; the elderly with no support network to help them through tough times; families struggling with teen rebellion.

How can we change this downward spiral? How can we meet the needs of people who are trapped in a lifestyle of sin or who suffer the consequences of an immoral and uncaring community?

The answer lies in reaching out—from one heart to another. That's the spirit of life sharing. By inviting neighbors into our homes and letting them see how we live and love, we can show how our relationship with God makes a difference. When we warmly invite neighbors in for a meal, a cup of coffee, or to enjoy a party, they can see how we integrate Christian principles into our friendships, marriage, and family responsibilities. And most important, our open doors will give us the right and opportunity to share with them the greatest news we have ever received—that God loves us and wants to have a relationship with us through His Son, Jesus Christ.

Although many of us do not think we have the gift of evangelism, we all have God-given strengths and talents that He wants to use in bringing forth His fruit. Life sharing allows us to develop these abilities. It also gives us opportunities to present the gospel in a clear, nonthreatening way to those who desperately need a touch from our loving heavenly Father.

Over the years, Barbara and I have met many people who lack confidence in their ability to witness. Some have tried and failed. Others have not known how to begin. But what excitement arises when these friends experience the joy and fulfillment of hosting a life-sharing event. "I can do that!" is what we hear over and over. "Why didn't someone tell me how easy this is before now?"

I urge you to let God work uniquely in your life. He wants to make you His partner in reaching others. In the words of Jesus, "I no longer call you servants, because a servant does not know his master's business. Instead, I have called you friends, for everything that I learned from my Father I have made known to you. You did not choose me, but I chose you and appointed you to go and bear fruit—fruit that will last" (John 15:15,16). I thank God for this privilege and give Him the freedom to work through me—in His own way and in His Spirit's power.

The renowned author Leo Tolstoy wrote, "History is shaped by the passions of the masses—the dreams, visions, and great ideas that seize the hearts and minds of men." That's our prayer for you—that God will give you a passion for your neighbors, dreams of introducing them to our Lord, and creative ideas on how to reach them through life sharing.

Perhaps you might concentrate on bringing together people who have similar interests, such as medical professionals, teachers, homemakers, parents of teens, or mothers of preschoolers. Whatever you choose to do, follow God's leading. And come alongside your Christian friends to hold each other accountable and pray together. As you do, God will use you to inspire the "passions" of many others to develop Biblical values that bring healing in your community.

As you make yourself available to our heavenly Father, we trust that the fruits of your ministry will spread beyond your neighborhood into your community—and perhaps even influence the world. And you will discover that evangelism really can be fun!

Resources
for Effective
Life
Sharing

Planning Schedule

WHAT	WHEN	HOW
1. Pray and start planning.		
2. Confirm your speaker.		
3. Train your helpers.		
4. Plan your follow-up.		
5. Send out invitations.		
6. Set up the event.		
7. Host the event.		
8. Help guests come to know Christ.		
9. Follow-up on those who respond.		
10. Evaluate your event.		

Hostess Checklist

What to do	The responsible party or decision made	✓
1. Set date for the event.		
2. Ask friends, neighbors, others to help you write invitations, provide table decorations and name tags, prepare refreshments, and serve as greeters. Then ask your helpers to suggest people to invite.		
3. Where will the event be held? What time?		
4. Who will the speaker be?		
5. Invitations: What kind? Who will write and send them? Who will call the people on the invitation list?		
6. Room preparations: Babysitting arrangements Someone to answer the telephone What to do with your pets Table to hold name tags Sign for the front door		
7. Prayer for the event. Ask your church to pray also.		

Personal Testimony Preparation Guidelines

Your personal testimony is a natural introduction into sharing the gospel of Christ. Use the following guidelines to help you develop your own story of what God has done in your life.

1. *Let God be original in you.* You are a unique person in God's eyes! You have your own story. In telling what Jesus Christ has done for you, He will be lifted up and glorified.

2. *Thank God for using you to introduce others to Jesus.* God's power shows up best in "weak" people. Read 1 Corinthians 2:1–5 and thank God for using you through His Spirit.

3. *Pray for wisdom.* Ask God to give you insight into how He has worked in your life.

4. *Consider your testimony as a one-to-one conversation.* Even if you'll be sharing your testimony with a group, think of it as talking to an individual. Prepare your story as a person who has the riches of Christ and wants to share them with another person.

5. *As you write, avoid Christian terminology.* Non-Christians are not familiar with biblical language. If you need to use religious terms, explain them. Also, avoid using denominational words.

6. *Guide your testimony around Paul's Before/How/After outline.* Read Acts 22, 23, and 26. Underline each part of the outline. Then complete the following outline parts.

❧ **Before** I received Christ, I lived and thought this way: Spend a brief time on the "before" part of the outline. Begin with how you became aware of the claims of Christ or first heard of His love for you. If you became a Christian as a child, thank God for the years you have known Him. What He has done for you is exciting, and people want to hear about that.

- **How** I received Christ:

  When relating your experience, be as specific as possible. The Holy Spirit often convinces people that they should receive Christ when they hear how someone else took that step. If you can't remember the exact time or circumstances of when you received Christ, give the general description.

- **After:** Begin with, *"Now that Christ is in my life and I am trusting Him, I live and think this way:"*

  Be practical and realistic as you explain how you are growing in your Christian life. Don't create the illusion that everything in your life is perfect. Describe how Christ has helped you solve your problems and met your insufficiencies. Some areas you may describe are:

  - Relationships with spouse, children, boss, employees, neighbors, or others
  - Atmosphere in your home
  - Adjusting to your new life
  - Your goals in life, your new priorities
  - Your inner peace
  - The bad habits God has enabled you to conquer
  - How you surrendered your daily life to God
  - Your new attitudes

  Be positive. Explain how you are applying God's Word to your life. Some ideas are:

  - God's love and forgiveness
  - Your sense of fulfillment
  - Freedom from fear
  - Assurance of eternal life
  - New purpose for living
  - Counsel from God's Word
  - New understanding for others
  - Your surrender to God as Lord and Master

Personal Testimony Worksheet

(For those who received Christ as an adult)

Use this worksheet to outline your testimony. Once you have a basic outline, it will be easier to complete the body of the testimony.

A beginning, attention-getting sentence:

Before I received Christ, I lived and thought this way:

How I received Christ:

After I received Christ, these changes took place:

A pertinent or favorite verse with which I can close my testimony:

Personal Testimony Worksheet

(For those who became a Christian at an early age)

Use this worksheet to outline your testimony. Once you have a basic outline, it will be easier to complete the body of the testimony.

A beginning, attention-getting sentence:

My background and early Christian experience:

My life between my early experience and when I yielded my life to Christ:

How I yielded my life to Christ:

After I yielded my life to Christ, these changes took place:

A pertinent or favorite verse with which I can close my testimony:

Personal Testimony Evaluation

1. What positive benefits were emphasized in the testimony?

2. Did the testimony avoid or explain terms that would not be understood by a non-Christian? If not, which terms were not explained?

3. Is the testimony so simple and clear that a non-Christian could receive Christ as a result of hearing it? If not, which areas were too complex or unclear?

4. Is the testimony honest or does it sound as if the Christian has such a problem-free life since receiving Christ that it appears to be unreal? How could the testimony be more realistic?

5. How can the testimony be improved?

Sample Follow-Up Letter

This is a sample letter you can send to someone who received Christ during your life-sharing event. Add your own personal comments.

(Your address and phone number)   *(Current date)*

Dear _____,

I enjoyed meeting you on *(insert the day you met)* and sharing with you about the good news of God's love and forgiveness. Your decision to receive Christ as your personal Savior and Lord is the greatest decision you have ever made.

In case you are wondering if Jesus is in your life right now, let me remind you that His Word promises He will never leave you (1 John 5:11–13). Isn't it wonderful to know He lives within you and has given you eternal life?

I trust you have experienced the sense of freedom and peace that Jesus gives. Remember that God loves you more than you love yourself, and He wants the very best for your life. Spiritual progress comes through allowing Him to change our attitudes and desires as He lives and works within us.

I welcome any questions you may have about your new Christian life. Several friends and I are beginning a new Bible study to learn more about God's will for our lives. We'd love to have you join us. Please call and let me know if you are available.

Be assured that I'm praying for you.

Your friend,

(Your Name)

Scheduling and Conducting a Follow-Up Appointment

Follow-Up for New Christians (Those Who Placed an "X" on the Comment Card)

1. Call and set a time to visit together.
2. During the appointment, share about yourself and how you began to grow in your Christian life. If the person understands that you are excited about your relationship with God, he or she probably will be interested in joining the Bible study and in meeting with you later.
3. If the new Christian agrees to attend the Bible study, provide a copy of the material that will be used. Review the Contents page to show what will be studied.

Follow-Up for the Person Who Seemed Open But Didn't Mark an "X"

Many people who attend an evangelistic event will not receive Christ at that time, but will be open to do so later. Sometimes just a few minutes together to answer their questions will be all the person needs to place his or her faith in Christ.

1. Call and set a time to visit together.
2. Ask for his or her impressions of your life-sharing event.
3. Review the *Four Spiritual Laws* with the person to give another opportunity to receive Christ.
4. Answer questions and be available to help meet needs.
5. Build a friendship by suggesting that you meet for lunch or another social occasion.

Tips for Handling a Follow-Up Telephone Call

1. Prepare for the call:
   * Contact the person as soon as possible after the event.

- Determine when you are available to meet with each person you will call.
- Set aside a block of time (one hour minimum) for calling. This allows for call-backs and helps you maintain concentration and a prayerful attitude.
- Briefly review the comment card information to familiarize yourself with the person.
- Bathe each call in prayer.

2. Conduct the telephone conversation:
- Be friendly and casual, but maintain your objective—setting up an appointment.
- Develop a telephone technique that works well but doesn't sound mechanical. Confidence will grow with preparation and experience.
- Relax. Assume that the person wants to meet with you.
- Identify yourself and your relationship with the host. You might say, *"I am a friend of _____ who hosted the coffee where we heard _____ speak."*
- Have your calendar ready. Suggest a time and place. Have alternative times available in case the first doesn't work. Preselect a location that is relatively free from distractions.
- If the person doesn't want to meet with you, don't press. Some people may not be ready to take this step.
- Avoid spiritual discussions over the phone. Your objective is to meet in person to discuss her relationship with Christ.
- Close the conversation by reviewing the meeting place, date, and time. Then say, *"I'm looking forward to meeting with you."*

3. Sample script for a telephone call:

Hi, this is Frances Follow-up, and I'm a friend of Harriet Host. You and I attended the same coffee when Terri Testimony spoke. (Mention information that the person included on his or her comment card.)

I was wondering if we can get together for lunch on Friday the 16th at 12:30. I'd like to get your feedback about the coffee.

Great, why don't I meet you at the Buttery Bakery on 10th Street. (Repeat the day, time, and restaurant before hanging up.)

4. Handling objections:

   ❧ "I'm a member of XYZ church already."

   That's great. It sounds like you're quite active. I think everyone should belong to a church! Why don't we get together and discuss what we heard about our relationship with God? Are you free on (repeat the date) *or would another time be better for you?*

   ❧ "I'm too busy."

   Yes, it is hard to find time to do extra things. But if we could meet briefly for lunch or another time that's convenient for you, I think we could have a meaningful time discussing what we heard. I don't want to push you, but I do want to be available.

5. Following the telephone call:

   ❧ If the appointment is more than a week away or the person seemed uncertain about meeting, write a brief note confirming the appointment.

   ❧ If the person wasn't antagonistic but couldn't meet with you, send a note expressing disappointment and openness to meet in the future. Enclose your testimony and perhaps a *Four Spiritual Laws* booklet. Record the date of your conversation, and follow through with an invitation to another event. Keep in touch until that person either meets with you or closes the door on your relationship.

The Follow-Up Appointment

1. Prepare for the meeting:

   ❧ Ask the Holy Spirit to fill you with wisdom and power.

   ❧ Relax and remember that witnessing is simply taking the initiative to share the gospel in the power of the Holy Spirit and leaving the results to God.

   ❧ Take two *Four Spiritual Laws* booklets with you.

   ❧ Be sensitive to the time limitations of the person you are meeting. Wrap up your meeting in about an hour.

2. Establish rapport:
   * Smile frequently.
   * Be friendly and warm.
   * Talk about the other person rather than yourself. Ask open-ended questions that take more than a "yes" or "no" answer.
3. Transition to a discussion of spiritual matters:
   * Ask thought-provoking questions such as, "What did you think of what you heard at the coffee?" or "Did what the speaker said make sense to you?" or "Where are you on your spiritual journey?" or "How would you describe your relationship with God right now?"
   * Listen carefully to the person's answers to gain insight into his or her attitudes and spiritual condition. This knowledge will help you choose what to emphasize in your gospel presentation and to make sure your contact is ready for a commitment.
   * Share the *Four Spiritual Laws* booklet. If your friend has already heard the presentation at the life-sharing event, ask questions to clarify where she stands spiritually and where Christ is in relation to her right now. If the person is hesitant, suggest reviewing the booklet to help determine what is keeping her from making a commitment to Christ.
   * If the person knows that Christ is in her life, review the sections on assurance, promises, feelings, benefits, and growth on pages 11–15 of the booklet.
4. Close the appointment:
   * If the person received Christ in prayer, invite her to your Bible study.
   * If the person is not a Christian, invite her to the Bible study anyway. Sometimes it takes more exposure to God's Word before an unbeliever can trust Christ.
   * Suggest that your new friend read the Gospel of John.
   * Encourage her to call you with any questions, or concerns, or just to get to know each other better.

How to Lead a Small Group Bible Study

Personal preparation is a vital first step. Be sure that Christ is Lord of your life and that you are filled with the Holy Spirit. I encourage you to read these booklets: the *Four Spiritual Laws* and *Have You Made the Wonderful Discovery of the Spirit-Filled Life?* They contain the basic principles you will need to live a victorious Christian life and be an effective leader of your group. You can obtain them from your local Christian bookstore, your mail-order distributor, or NewLife Publications.

Next, pray for God's leading and blessing. Then invite your friends or announce plans for your Bible study group to people at your job or in your dormitory or neighborhood. Often those to whom you have witnessed and who have received Christ as Savior in your life-sharing event will be interested in participating.

Select the material you will use during your study. We recommend *Five Steps of Christian Growth*, which includes five simple lessons that will present the gospel, help new believers receive an assurance of their salvation, and show them how to grow in their faith. The leader's and student guides are available also from your local Christian bookstore, your mail-order distributor, or NewLife Publications.

Choose the people you think would be more interested; pray about them individually; then visit each one personally. After you make the contacts, select a meeting place and time for your Bible study.

Keep your group small. With eight to twelve people, group members will feel freer to interact and discuss the lesson material. You will also be able to give your students more individual attention as they begin to apply biblical truths in their lives.

Be sure your meeting location is neat, attractive, and well-ventilated, and free from interruption. If several days lapse between your initial contact and the first Bible study, remind those who have expressed interest. Make an announcement, speak to them personally, phone them, or send cards.

Avoid pressuring anyone to join your group. At the same time, do not have a negative or apologetic attitude. The best way to promote interest and enthusiasm is to be interested and enthusiastic yourself. Let me suggest some approaches.

> "John, you've expressed an interest in learning how to share your faith in Christ. (Show him Lesson 1.) This has been a tremendous help to me in learning about the Bible in a short time. I think it could be a real help to both of us if we studied together."

or

> "John, several of us are getting together to study about sharing our faith with others. We believe that, if we do it as a group, we will all benefit. Why don't you join us?"

As you pray and wait on God, He will lead you to those He has chosen for your study.

Your Bible study group may consist of Christians at different levels of spiritual maturity. A few may already be familiar with some of the content while for others it will be completely new. The informal nature of a small group study is ideal for helping students learn from each other as well as from the things you say.

Guidelines for Leading

When leading the Bible study sessions, follow these guidelines:

- Create an informal atmosphere so you and your group can get to know each other. Address each person by name. Introduce new members before the discussion begins. Contact visitors during the week and invite them to return for the next session. Pray daily for each person in your group.

- Have your Bible open at all times. If your students are unfamiliar with the Bible, offer to help them find Scripture verses and allow time for them to locate the passages in their own Bibles. If a student does not have a Bible, help him obtain one. Bring extra Bibles and pencils for students to use during the study time.

* Be yourself. Depend on the Holy Spirit to work through the person you are, not through some artificial "spiritual leader" image you think you should project.

* Don't be bound to your notes. Maintain eye contact with your group.

* A group leader is a discussion guide, not a lecturer. Rather than dominating the discussion, draw out comments from your students. Be prepared to suggest ideas, give background material, and ask questions to keep the conversation lively and relevant. If a student is saying something productive and to the point, refrain from inserting your own thoughts. When he finishes, guide, clarify, and summarize. Keep the discussion centered on the principle passages of Scripture. Encourage silent members of the group to get involved in the discussion.

* When you ask a question, allow time for students to think before continuing. Then listen to their answers rather than mentally planning what you are going to say next. Remember, you are teaching people, not lessons.

* Make sure everyone understands the major points in the lesson.

* Get involved in the lives of your group members. Communicating the basic truths of the Christian life is more than passing on information; it is sharing life experiences. Help them put into practice the truths you are teaching. The way you model and mentor through your personal example will have a far greater impact on your group than any of the words you say in a meeting.

* Plan extra time for taking your students witnessing and for informal times of fellowship. The lessons will tell you how and when to conduct these activities.

Remember that each group has its own personality. Some groups are active, others more subdued. Adapt your leadership style to fit your group. But remember—your most important quality as a leader is to be open to the Holy Spirit's guidance as you help your students apply the lessons they are learning.

How to Encourage Participation

Your objective in these Bible studies is to help develop spiritual maturity among group members and train them to introduce others to Christ. Your main activity should be studying the Scriptures, and any discussion should follow the study lesson plan. To encourage participation, sit in a circle. Ideally, to avoid losing a feeling of intimacy, no group should have more than twelve people. When your group exceeds that number, you may want to divide into two groups.

Here are some suggestions for encouraging members to participate and for making the discussion time interesting and practical:

* Ask the group to read the Bible passage to be discussed, with each person reading one verse aloud. Invite one member to summarize the passage in his own words before asking any questions about it.

* When discussing the study questions, ask specific students to answer them. Avoid embarrassing anyone. When you ask a question of a member, be sure he answers it aptly. If he stumbles, help him along and make him feel that he did answer the question, at least in part. Compliment him on his response.

* If you sense confusion about a question you ask, restate it in different words or from another point of view.

* After one person has made a point, ask others if they agree. Have them state their reasons. Often a great deal can be learned by disagreeing over a passage. To keep the discussion from turning into an argument, remind everyone that you are studying what the Bible says about a subject.

* At the end of the discussion, ask someone to summarize the points that have been made. Be sure to guide the final summary and application.

* If a person asks a question that is off the topic, tactfully explain that it would be best not to take class time to discuss it. Offer to help answer the question personally after the study session is over.
* Define all unusual words.
* Keep the discussion relevant and personal. Avoid arguments. Don't let one person dominate the discussion. To redirect the discussion, restate the question or ask for the answers to the next question.
* To stimulate discussion, ask such questions as: "What do you think this passage means?" "What can we learn from this passage about God, Christ, ourselves, our responsibility, our relationships with others?"
* Help the students apply the passage personally. Ask, "What significance does this have for us today?" "What does this mean to you?" "How does (or will) it affect your life?" Talk about the witnessing experiences your students have had during the past week.
* Keep the discussion moving. If you go through the material too quickly, the study will be shallow; if you go too slowly, it will seem tedious and boring. The lessons may include more material than you need. Don't spend too much time on any one section, but be sure you cover each major point.
* Be punctual about beginning and closing the session.
* Make the group activity enjoyable. Allow extra time after the study for individual counseling, social interaction, and/or refreshments.

Speaker's Worksheet

Use this worksheet to write out the parts of your talk other than your personal testimony. As you practice your talk, refer to what you have written on this worksheet until you can repeat it without looking.

Introduction to establish rapport:
    Acknowledge the introduction that was made about you.

    Give a humorous story or situation to put the audience at ease.

    Repeat the title of your message.

Sharing of your personal testimony (Attach a copy of your personal testimony worksheet.)

Two illustrations of how God specifically worked in your everyday life (Give Christ the credit rather than your hard work or better circumstances.)

Transition into the *Four Spiritual Laws*

Invitation for listeners to pray if they desire

Transition to the comment cards

Closing comments

How to Present the Four Spiritual Laws

The *Four Spiritual Laws* is not the only way to share your faith with a group. But to hundreds of thousands, it has proved to be an effective evangelism tool. The book's positive tone, its brevity, its simple gospel presentation, and the clear section on how to receive Christ all combine to make this an effective evangelistic tool.

Benefits of using the *Four Spiritual Laws* in a group:

1. It presents the claims of Christ clearly.
2. It enables you to be brief, prepared, and confident.
3. It helps you stay on the subject.
4. It includes an invitation to receive Christ.
5. It offers suggestions for growth and emphasizes the importance of the church.
6. It can be left with each member of your group.
7. It is an immediate follow-up tool.

Purpose of the circle diagrams:

1. To further clarify why people need Christ.
2. To help a person recognize his own relationship with God.

The main purpose of the circle diagrams is to help group members discern where they are in relationship with Christ. Your goal is to read and explain the diagrams clearly and move on to the prayer on the next page. The prayer is where each person will have an opportunity to respond to the gospel. The circles merely help bring the nonbeliever to that point. Be careful not to bog down at this point but keep your presentation moving.

Principles for presenting the booklet:

1. Give a booklet to each person.

2. Use a transition like this one:

   "I would like to give each of you a booklet that has been very helpful to me. I would like to go over the contents for two reasons. First, you may know what you believe but do not know how to share your faith with others. Second, perhaps some of you are wondering how you can have a personal relationship with Christ."

3. Read the booklet as guests follow along in their copies.

4. Give an opportunity to receive Christ in prayer.

   * Read through the suggested prayer.

   * Read the question and statement immediately following the prayer.

   * Invite your listeners who had never invited Jesus into their life to pray silently with you as you read the prayer aloud again, phrase by phrase.

   * This is a sample invitation to receive Christ in prayer:

   "For many of you, this prayer will express the desire of your heart. Let me suggest that, if you are not sure that Christ is in your life, we pray together so you can be sure. Pray silently, repeating after me as I pray aloud. Let's pray. (Then pray a sentence at a time, pausing for them to follow your lead.)

5. Read the booklet through page 15.

6. Give everyone present a 3×5 card and ask them to write these items:

   * Name, address, and phone number

   * Any comments or questions they may have

   * An "X" by their name if they have just invited Christ into their life for the first time

7. Ask listeners to fold cards in half and leave them in a convenient location.[1]

---

[1] Further training in personal evangelism is available through Lay Institute for Evangelism given by ChurchLife, a ministry of Campus Crusade for Christ.

Invitations and Menu Ideas

Centerpiece Ideas

- ❧ A large plant from your home with a bow to match your decor
- ❧ Small or large figurines
- ❧ Large table books, such as ones for flower arranging or geographical photography books, that fit the occasion
- ❧ Set the figurines or plant on top of large table books
- ❧ A hollowed-out pumpkin filled with a dried flower arrangement
- ❧ Framed pictures and poems
- ❧ Special plates on plate holders
- ❧ A large bowl or basket filled with colorful fruit or vegetables
- ❧ Votive candles in 2 or 3 large candleholders
- ❧ A picnic basket with a plant inside
- ❧ Any treasure you have in your home, such as antique dishes, knickknacks, fancy hats
- ❧ A collection of shells, dolls, teacups, or thimbles
- ❧ A cowboy hat with one boot and a lariat
- ❧ A straw hat with a colored ribbon
- ❧ An arrangement of flowers
- ❧ A basket filled with herb plants

A Delightful Easter Brunch

Centerpiece

Put a dozen brown and white eggs in a basket. Decorate with a large bouquet of parsley in tufts by eggs.

Menu

- ✽ Quesadilla quiche[2]
- ✽ Frosted fruit cocktail[2]
- ✽ Angel biscuits[2]
- ✽ Bran muffins
- ✽ Coffee cake
- ✽ Coffee/tea/juice

Greet your guests with orange juice.

A Delightful Easter Brunch

Let's celebrate together on
Saturday, April 10
10:30 a.m.

in the home of our neighbor, Sue Ross
330 Gladstone Circle

"Easter Is More Than Bunnies and Eggs" will
be shared by Ruth Davis, a friend from Atlanta.

R.S.V.P. 345-7285

An Informal Coffee

Schedule during either the morning or afternoon.

Menu

- ✽ Coffee/tea/hot chocolate
- ✽ Coffee cake/bread/muffins   *or*
- ✽ Donuts from a bakery shop
- ✽ Fruit cup   *or*
- ✽ A mix of raisins, nuts, and bits of dried fruit to nibble on

---

[2] Recipe included in *Joy of Hospitality Cookbook*

Neighbors!
A Time to Sit Down and Catch Up!

Tuesday, January 10
10:00 a.m.
Anne Linns—36 Devonshire

Stop by as we chat and listen to a talk on
"Christianity in a Woman's World"
by Carol Gustafson

A Valentine's Day Dinner

Barbara:

Enjoy a small dinner party to build bridges to evangelism. Six or eight guests allows for good discussion around the table. Invite one Christian couple and four new guests. Set the scene with background music and candlelight, including tall, votive, and floating candles. Serve simple gourmet food. (Most people have the mistaken idea that gourmet food has to be complicated. Not so. Some of the best gourmet recipes are simple to make and serve.) Take treasures from your home and maybe a plant or two to make a centerpiece. Making sure it is low enough that the guests can converse over it. Here is one example of what I do for this dinner.

Centerpiece
Angels, red candles, and an ivy plant or bouquet

Place settings
If you do not have a set of expensive china, you can mix and match plates and goblets for an eclectic look.

Simple menu

- Entre and salad with touches of red in them, such as red onions, red gelatin, red apples, or red grapes
- Chocolate cake with raspberries spooned over each slice

Elaborate menu

- Mushrooms stuffed with spinach and cheese
- Black raspberry glazed chicken breasts with wild rice and almond stuffing[3]
- Rolls
- Romaine, red onion, and orange salad
- Bittersweet chocolate fudge cake with chocolate cream frosting served with raspberries

"It Takes Two to Tango"

We would like to invite you to a Valentine's Day dinner to meet our friends, Ken and Mary Mann who will share "It Takes Two to Tango," a fun but practical message on their marriage relationship.

Time: 6:30 p.m.

Date: February 14

Place: 2627 Lakeshore Drive

Given by Sam and Alice Wainwright

Please R.S.V.P. at 328-2112

---

[3] Recipe included in *Joy of Hospitality Cookbook*

Appetizer Buffet

Ask guests to bring their favorite appetizer with recipe. Greet them with punch served from a separate table. Reserve the large table for all the appetizers. Your appetizer may be a cutting tray with a variety of cheeses, such as goat, cheddar, brie, swiss, and gruyère. Men love this! Provide knives to cut the cheeses.

Use a table runner or large tablecloth. Set out paper plates or salad plates. Choose a special dessert such as a trifle[4] or a cake trio such as white, chocolate, and spice. Also provide coffee and tea.

You are invited to a
Neighborhood Appetizer Buffet

at

Bill and Anne Smith's home
1245 Normandy Lane
Saturday, March 10
7:00 p.m.

We would like you to come for appetizers and dessert, some laughs, and a chance to meet old and new neighbors as well as to meet some special friends, Rose and Omar Sutherland. During the evening, they will share their thoughts on "How Do You Spell Relief? A Biblical Perspective on Handling Stress and Anxiety."

We are excited about this buffet and look forward to seeing you.

R.S.V.P. 338-3387

P.S. Please bring an appetizer to serve 12.

---

[4] Recipe included in *Joy of Hospitality Cookbook*

Dessert Event

Invite your guests in for dessert. You might serve:

- Coconut cake[5], Viennese chocolate cake[5], and carrot cake
- Trifle[5]
- Sugar cookies
- Fruit in season (whole apples, pears, and bananas)
- Assorted nuts or a dried fruit combination
- A special box of candy

If you serve fresh fruit, slice it on a tray and sprinkle lemon juice over fruit to prevent browning. This menu can easily be doubled for a larger crowd. The trifle bowl should take the place of honor at the table. Serve with different flavored coffees, including decaffeinated and regular, and a simple punch bowl.

This event works well during the Christmas season.

Off the Diet—For One Night!

Come join us for dessert
June 10th at 7:00 p.m.

Our friends, Jim and Amy Wilson will share with us
"How God Made Our Two Hearts One."

Love,

Tom and Sue Pagel
213 Happy Rock Road

Please R.S.V.P. 886-5454

---

[5] Recipe included in *Joy of Hospitality Cookbook*

The Wordless Book:
Lesson for Children

The Wordless Book is a time-tested method of teaching children about the wonderful love of Jesus. Even young children can remember the colors and what they stand for in the gospel story. Study the lesson carefully so you can present the material without looking at notes or at this book. When teaching this lesson, invite the children to participate as much as possible. Remember these directions for using this lesson: Directions for the teacher are in normal type; answers to questions are in parentheses and italicized; and words to say to students are in bold type.

The Preparation

Using brightly colored construction paper, cut one 4-inch square each of yellow, black, red, white, and green. Stack the squares in the order listed, then staple them together on the left-hand edge to make a book. Make enough Wordless Books to give each child in your class a copy. If you have enough time during the lesson, you may ask the children to cut out the colored squares and staple their own books. Mark Scripture references on slips of paper like this:

Yellow: John 3:16
John 10:10

Black: Romans 3:23
Romans 6:23

Red: Romans 5:8,9
Matthew 1:211
Corinthians 15:3,4
John 14:6

White: Ephesians 2:8,9
John 1:12

Green: Hebrews 13:5
2 Peter 3:18

Use a version of the Bible that is easy for children to understand. Use the slips of paper to mark the references you'll read during the lesson. You may also want to order the *Good News Comic Book* to help you lead a child to Christ. The booklet explains God's plan of salvation in the same way that it is presented in this lesson. The comic book can be used individually with children as you counsel them, and the child can then take the booklet home.

To order, ask for it at your Christian bookstore or see the Resource page at the back of this book.

The Lesson

When you are ready to teach the lesson, ask the children to sit in a semi-circle around you. Say: **Have you ever seen a book without words? Today, we're going to hear a story from a Wordless Book.**

Hand each child a book, or just hold up your own book. Then say: **This book tells a wonderful story of good news. Do you like to hear good news? Yes, everyone does.**

Hold up the front of your book to display the yellow page. Say: **The first page of our book is yellow. What does yellow remind you of?** *(Sunlight, brightness, the sun.)*

This yellow page tells us that God has a wonderful plan for our lives. Let me explain. Yellow reminds me of light. God wants us to live in light, not in darkness. The Bible tells us that God is light. He wants to light our way so we can do what's right and good.

Yellow also reminds me of heaven. God wants us to live in heaven with Him some day. The Bible says: (Read John 3:16, then say:) **When God says He loves the world, that means you and me. God's Son, Jesus Christ, left heaven to live on earth. He said:** (Read John 10:10.)

This is Good News! But not all boys and girls have this joyful, happy life.

Turn to the black page. Then say: **This dark page tells us why. It says that every man, woman, boy, and girl has sinned and is separated from God.** (Read Romans 3:23.)

That is why we can't know God or enjoy God's wonderful plan for us.

Ask: **What is sin?** *(Doing wrong things, hitting, swearing, etc.)*

Say: **Sin is not knowing God or caring about Him. Sin is wanting to have our own way, not God's way. Have you ever told a lie? Been unkind? Disobeyed your parents? Cheated? Hated anyone? Stolen anything? People do these things because they are sinful and separated from God.**

Turn back to the yellow page. Then say: **Since God is light,** (turn to the black page) **and we are in darkness because of our sin, we are separated from God. The Bible says:** (Read Romans 6:23.) **This kind of death means spiritual separation from God. This isn't good news, is it? Then how can this be a Good News story?**

Turn to the red page. Say: **The red page tells us about how Jesus shed His blood for us.** (Read Romans 5:8,9.) **This verse says that Jesus was punished for our sins. He took our place! He could do this because He did not sin. He didn't have anything to pay for Himself.**

How did this happen? At Christmas, we celebrate the birth of Jesus. Jesus is God. He was living in heaven, but He came to earth as a baby. Why did He come? (Read Matthew 1:21.)

At Easter, we remember that Jesus died on the cross. But He didn't have to die. He is God. He could have gotten off the cross at any time. But He let Himself be nailed to the cross. He did this because He loves us so much. After He died, Jesus was buried. Then He came alive again. (Read 1 Corinthians 15:3,4.) **Now Jesus lives forever! That's why Jesus can say:** (Read John 14:6.)

This is Good News! But it is not enough just to know these three things:

Turn to the yellow page. Say: **God loves me.**

Turn to the black page. Say: **I have sinned.**

Turn to the red page. Say: **Jesus died and came alive for me.**

Turn to the white page. Say: **This page tells us that we can have a new, clean life.**

All each of us needs to do is believe that Jesus is God, and that He died to pay for our sins, then ask Him to forgive us of our sins and become our Savior.

This new life is God's greatest gift to us. Do you like gifts? You can receive God's greatest gift right now. The Bible says: (Read Ephesians 2:8,9.)

Then say: **If I handed you a gift right now, would you say, "No, thank you; I don't want it"? No, you would take it. The gift wouldn't be yours until you took it. Jesus Christ is God's free gift to us. This is how you can receive it. Talk to God right now. Talking to God is called prayer. You can say something like this:**

"Dear God, I know that I have sinned. I want to have a clean, new life. I want to receive Jesus into my life as my Savior. Please forgive me of my sins. Thank You that Jesus is in my life right now. Amen."

If you pray words like those and really mean it, Jesus will come into your life. He will help you have a new, joyful life. Would you like to pray this prayer right now? Remember, it isn't the words you say that are important, but the attitude of your heart.

Ask the children to bow their heads. Then say: **If you want to ask Jesus into your life, say these words with me.** Repeat the prayer, then ask:

Did you receive Jesus as your Savior? Then where is He right now? *(In my life.)*

Say: **God gives us a promise in His Word.** (Read John 1:12.) **Would God tell a lie? No, of course not! If you received Jesus into your life, you are a child of God.**

So far, we have learned four things. Turn to the pages and say the words with me:

Turn to the yellow page. Say: **God loves me.**

Turn to the black page. Say: **I have sinned.**

Turn to the red page. Say: **Jesus died and came alive for me.**

Turn to the white page. Say: **When I receive Jesus, I am forgiven and become a child of God.**

Say: **God always loves you and keeps His promises. He has promised:** (Read Hebrews 13:5.) **Let's say this together. "I will never leave you."**

Turn to the green page. Say: **But we have one page left. What does green remind you of?** *(Trees, grass.)*

Say: **Green reminds me of growing things. You are growing right now. But just as your body is growing, your new spirit needs to grow, too. Growing in your spirit means becoming and acting more like Jesus.** (Read 2 Peter 3:18.) **This is how we grow spiritually:**

1. **We talk to God (pray).**
2. **We read God's Word, the Bible.**
3. **We practice the good works we read about in the Bible.**
4. **We go to church to hear more about Jesus.**
5. **We tell others about God's Good News.**

Say: **I'm so glad you came to my house today to hear about God's Good News. If you asked Jesus to be your Savior as I told the story, come and tell me after I pray. I want to hear about your exciting decision and give you something to help you grow in God's family.**

You may take your Wordless Book home with you. You can share God's Good News with others, too. Use your Wordless Book to tell many people about Jesus.

Close in prayer, asking God to protect each person and help the children learn more about Jesus. Thank those who helped you with your club. Then dismiss the children.

Other Resources to Help in Life Sharing

Ministries

Character Clubs

Children of the World, a ministry of Campus Crusade for Christ, helps adults win and disciple children through Character Clubs. To receive more information about the Character Clubs curriculum and training, write: Children of the World, 910 Calle Negocio, Suite 300, San Clemente, CA 92673.

Child Evangelism Fellowship Inc.

Child Evangelism Fellowship (CEF) helps adults lead children to Christ and grow in their faith through Bible clubs in homes and churches. Child Evangelism offers an array of materials for leaders. These resources are available through your local Christian bookstore or by calling your local CEF area director.

Student Venture

VITAL LINC is the volunteer-directed ministry of Student Venture, the high school outreach of Campus Crusade for Christ. Its purpose is to help volunteers bring Christ to students on campuses in their own communities. A key person is "coached" by a Student Venture staff member over the telephone or through the mail. For more information, please call (800) 789-5462.

LIFE Conferences

LIFE (Lay Institute for Evangelism) conferences are a combination of lectures and small group seminars presented by ChurchLIFE, a ministry of Campus Crusade for Christ. The conferences give a foundation for a successful Christian walk in the power of the Holy Spirit. For information on how your church can sponsor a conference, call ChurchLIFE at (800) 873-5222.

Executive Ministry

Executive Ministries offers Christian executives, leaders, and influencers a unique opportunity to develop a personal ministry in evangelism and discipleship to peers in their community. For more information, call (407) 826-2475.

Christmas Gatherings

Christmas Gatherings is a ministry encouraging Christians to gather friends and neighbors in their homes during the holidays. To order your *Christmas Gatherings Resource Manual* or to receive training, write Christmas Gatherings, 24904 Logan Avenue, Lakeville, MN 55044 or call (612) 469-4793.

Books

Joy of Hospitality Cookbook. Vonette Bright and Barbara Ball, editors. A companion to the *Joy of Hospitality* book, the *Joy of Hospitality Cookbook* offers elegant and easy-to-serve menus by Campus Crusade for Christ staff and friends who have contributed their best recipes.

Witnessing Without Fear. Bill Bright. In this best-selling Gold Medallion book, Bill Bright offers simple step-by-step coaching on how to share your faith with confidence and provides specific answers to questions you will most often encounter in witnessing.

Five Steps to Sharing Your Faith. Bill Bright. This Bible study leader's guide and study guide will help you learn how to introduce your friends and loved ones to Jesus Christ. The study gives practical training on how to teach small group members to prepare a personal testimony, present the gospel simply and clearly, guide new believers to assurance of their salvation, and encourage fellowship in a good church.

Five Steps to Christian Growth. Bill Bright. This Bible study helps you discover what the Bible says about being sure of your salvation, experiencing God's love and forgiveness, being filled with the Holy Spirit, and much more. Leader's guide and study guide available.

Good News Comic Book. Introduce children to Christ with this colorful gospel story in comic book form. Ideal for Sunday school, vacation Bible school, and as bag stuffers for special children's events.

Good News Glove. A classic and fun tool to witness to children, this colorful glove helps children understand and remember the gospel. Each finger communicates a basic scriptural truth in an exciting and game-like manner that keeps kids' attention and hearts. Can be used alone or with the *Good News Comic Book*.

Four Spiritual Laws. This booklet presents a clear explanation of the gospel of Jesus Christ. One of the most effective evangelistic tools ever developed, the *Four Spiritual Laws* helps you open your conversation easily and share your faith with confidence.

Would You Like to Belong to God's Family? is a children's version of the *Four Spiritual Laws*. Help your little ones learn how to understand and receive God's love and forgiveness in Jesus Christ.

Would You Like to Know God Personally? This booklet presents four principles for establishing a personal relationship with God. This evangelistic tool will help you lead others to Christ so they can lead others to Him also.

Have You Made the Wonderful Discovery of the Spirit-Filled Life? Discover the Spirit-filled life and how to live in moment-by-moment dependence on God. Millions have learned to live an abundant life by following the simple truths found in this booklet.

Transferable Concepts. Bill Bright. These concepts offer principles that lead to a more effective witness and Christian walk. Available in booklet, video, and audio. Also available in Spanish.

> *How You Can Be Filled With the Holy Spirit*
> *How You Can Be Sure You Are a Christian*
> *How You Can Be a Fruitful Witness*
> *How You Can Walk in the Spirit*

Joy of Hospitality Kit. This practical kit includes all the resources you need to host a life-sharing demonstration event in your home or church, including invitations, a *Joy of Hospitality* book and cookbook, copies of the *Four Spiritual Laws,* and much more.

Videos

"JESUS" video. This realistic video on the life of Christ will help you introduce your friends, neighbors, and loved ones to the life, death, and resurrection of Jesus. Shot on location to give you the real-life flavor, feel, and sounds of where our Lord actually lived.

"JESUS" Home Video Package. This package is an effective strategy to reach your friends and neighbors for Christ. It includes a witnessing training video, the *"JESUS"* video, and resources to help you present the gospel and help new believers grow in their faith. To order, call New Life Resources at (800) 827-2788.

Reach Your World through Witnessing Without Fear. This video package provides the resources you need to more effectively share the gospel with everyone in your world. This proven evangelistic training tool is available in group and individual study versions.

The Total Package. This video package will help teens understand God's love and forgiveness and begin growing in their faith. The video includes appearances by well-known athletes and music from Christian celebrities. The package comes with a 60-minute video, magazine, and a special edition of *The Living Bible*.

A Man Without Equal video. Dr. Bill Bright explores the unique birth, earthly life, teaching, death, and resurrection of Jesus Christ and shows how Jesus continues to change the way we live and think today. The video provides a clear presentation of the gospel and gives an invitation to receive Christ.

Knowing God Personally video and magazine. This 60-minute instructional drama video is an excellent follow-up tool for Christians who desire to help their friends and neighbors begin growing in their new faith. Designed to be used with the *"JESUS"* video, the package includes an accompanying magazine that reinforces foundational biblical principles through a Bible study format.

These resources are available through your local Christian bookstore, mail-order catalog distributor, or order from New-Life Publications by calling (800) 235-7255. E-mail: Internet, newlife@magicnet.net; CompuServe, 74114,1206.

CALVARY BAPTIST CHURCH
Baker, Oregon 97814

Vonette Bright has assisted her husband, Dr. Bill Bright, in ministry for more than forty years. As co-founder of Campus Crusade for Christ, she has entertained friends and acquaintances from all walks of life, small and large groups, and heads of state.

An internationally known speaker and author, she currently directs Women Today, a radio and resource ministry that encourages women to take the next step of faith as they seek to influence their world.

Barbara Ball has entertained evangelistically in her home for more than thirty years. She is the co-author of several books and booklets on evangelistic entertaining. She and her husband, Howard, direct the ChurchLIFE Ministry of Campus Crusade for Christ, teaching laymen how to share their faith.